AN VALUES
AND HOW TO
FIGHT THEM

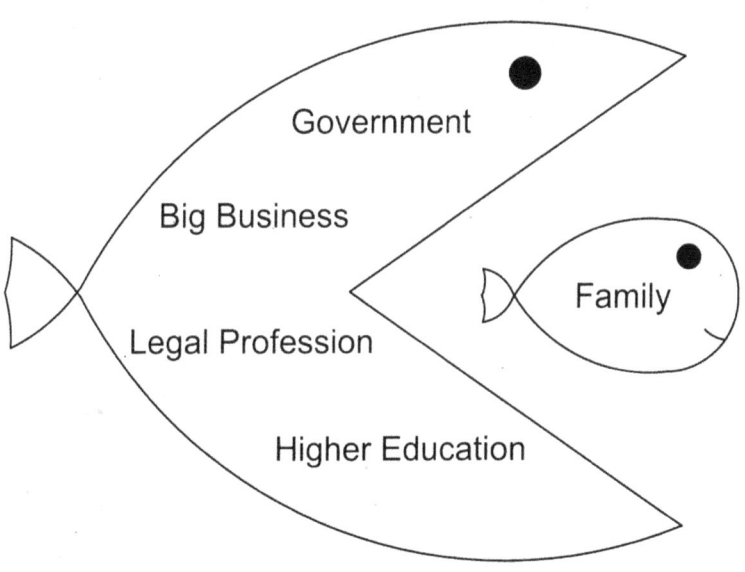

Government

Big Business

Legal Profession

Family

Higher Education

Thomas R Jarboe PhD

ISBN: 1-4392-4003-5
ISBN-13: 9781439240038

Visit www.booksurge.com to order additional copies.

Anti-Family Values and How to Fight Them

by

Thomas R. Jarboe Ph.D.

This book is dedicated to my Family.

Preface

Our free society, with free enterprise governed by a democratic system, is an extremely good environment for human existence and progress. However, because of that freedom, institutions within our society can become parasitic, growing and evolving to strengthen themselves at the expense and the extinction of our families. The characteristics of institutions with the strongest growth are spread through direct takeover of other institutions, copying by others, and eventual size dominance. This book explains how many of the anti-family values now being imposed on our society came about as the result of institutions evolving into family killers. Propaganda from such institutions instills values that cause families to allow the institutions to take their wealth and their children, extinguishing the family. As you shall see, Darwin's concepts of evolution apply to institutions even better than animals, for institutions can evolve much faster than animals.

An institution is any organization of people within society. Examples of institutions are churches, governments, government bureaucracies, and higher education. Institutions can have institutions within them. For example, higher education consists of universities, some of which consist of multiple colleges, all of which consist of multiple disciplines that are also institutions. The government is an institution that contains bureaucracies that are also institutions. Some of the most family-damaging values come from the competition for survival between the smaller institutions within the larger ones. By families I mean real human families, with parents and children, where the children are the offspring of the parents.

Families are the basis of the sustained existence of societies and are, therefore, the fundamental institution of humanity. Since families are the source of humanity they are the host institutions for all other human institutions. In order to survive, we must make sure the relationship of other institutions to families is symbiotic and not parasitic. Many of our institutions have evolved into parasites that are killing our best families through the instillation of family-extinguishing values that provide a short-term benefit to the institutions. However, they are causing a massive reduction in the next generation of top-quality children. In the long term, this killing of the host will lead to the death of the all institutions. We must develop synergistic relationships between families and institutions for both to do well. We must recognize that the family is the host and the other institutions are the parasites. We must work hard to make them beneficial parasites. Suggested changes in the rules for institutions, which will achieve this synergy, are given in this book. Higher education has evolved into one of the most damaging institutions (both to families and itself) and is in need of change.

The effects of family-extinguishing values are widespread. Divorce rates are outrageously high, and women are being forced out of the home and into the workplace. Traditionally male professions are being forced to include women, and the female professions must include men. Homosexual behavior is encouraged. Family-splitting male-hatemongering is widespread. Family-strengthening religions are under attack. The most talented and educable people are taught that having a large family is immoral, but our least talented people, unable to find high-paying jobs but able to receive aid to dependent children, are all but forced to have many children to survive. We are being told that humans are evil, the earth would be better off without them, and, therefore, killing them in the womb is good. The government is preventing its citizens from rearing children with the discipline they need to lead productive and happy lives. Completely out of control, bureaucracies exercise real power directly over families but answer to no one. The extinction of many families is the worst effect of these anti-children, anti-family values.

The power, wealth, and freedom of families are being attacked and usurped by the parasitic institutions. Taxes are getting higher and more complex, and family rights and freedoms are being reduced at a rapid rate. Ridiculous lawsuits are rampant, with lawyers becoming more and more of a burden on families while those they are supposed to defend see less and less benefit. Healthcare costs are skyrocketing. The Federal justice system does not work. Over half the people in jail are there for crimes against themselves. The police care more about their own safety, image, and visibility than about the safety of the people they are hired to protect. All the violence in the media leads Americans to think that violent crime is increasing, causing families to trade wealth and freedom for security, when in fact crime rates have been dropping dramatically.

Familiarizing itself with the concept of institution evolution allows the logical mind to understand a great deal of the absurdity around us. The human mind remains capable of logical thinking only when it is nurtured in an environment of mostly logical thinking. Unfortunately, a large number of the minds in American society have been rendered incapable, having been overexposed to the absurd ideas and morality that have been thrust upon them by the evolved parasitic institutions. Once we understand how institution evolution works, we will regain our sanity and change the rules so that organizations evolve to help our families, which should be their purpose. Humans are basically good, and most of the evil in the world is not due to evil people. Rather, it is due to our lack of understanding concerning the need to control institution evolution to benefit our families. This book attempts to improve that understanding.

Various evolved institutions, including higher education, the psychiatric profession, the criminal justice system, the U.S. government, and the legal profession, are examined herein. The evolutionary growth of destructive aspects of these valuable institutions will be discussed and corrective action suggested. Since human nature strongly impacts the way institutions evolve, the author's understanding of human nature and the difference between men and women are described in the Appendix. The assumption about human nature given in the Appendix and the assumption of institution evolution form the logical basis of this book. Chapter 9 summarizes the laws we need to change to make our institutions evolve toward helping our families rather than destroying them.

Couples are extinguishing their families if they are having fewer than three children or are raising children that lack the values, self-discipline, and skills needed to support and raise their own families. Remember, two children are not enough for replacement because some will die before they reach adulthood, some will not find a mate, and many will be effectively sterilized by accepting the anti-family values described in this book.

Contents

1. The Massive Extinction Caused by Higher Education

I am a professor in a top research university, and I believe in higher education. It is absolutely necessary to maximize the learning rate of all people, especially the young, in a society built on such a massive knowledge base as ours. I believe we should be devoting more resources to education at all levels. However, the institution of higher education has evolved in certain areas in a manner that has an extremely negative impact on our families. College graduates have fewer children than needed for the survival of their families. [*The Bell Curve*, by Richard J. Herrnstein and Charles Murray, p 349] We need to change the way the universities receive money so that they will evolve to aid the survival of alumni families instead of causing their extinction.

In our society the universities that are considered the best are the ones that happen to have the most money. Recently established, great universities (like Harvey Mudd) demonstrate the fact that money makes them great. A large bequest from a generous benefactor can establish an excellent university almost overnight. Presently, one major money source, especially for private universities, is alumni. The *US News and World Report* even uses the amount of alumni contributions as a criterion in ranking universities. To get the largest amount of money possible from the alumni, the university must educate the students so that they will accumulate wealth, while instilling values that, in the end, will cause the alumni to give much of what they accumulate to their alma mater. The universities that adopt the campus philosophy that returns the most money from the alumni are the ones that have the most resources and become the most influential. For example, Harvard is often considered the top university, and it does have the most money in endowments. The students educated in the top universities tend to become the professors in the rest of the universities, and the values that these professors learned become more or less universal.

Some aspects of this campus philosophy, while good for the university in the short-term, are very bad for the continuation of the students' families. Only in recent years has a large fraction of the population taken advantage of higher education. This has led to the acceptance by an increasingly larger and more dominating segment of our society of very family-extinguishing values. Most of our leaders and influential people are now college educated, so the institution evolution of higher education has a large, somewhat random, and sometimes very negative impact on our families. The first step in controlling this evolution is to recognize why it is happening.

To amass more money, the university needs to eliminate the competition for the alumni's wealth. The biggest competitors are their families and their religions. If the alumni do not have children and abandon their religions they are likely to give most of the wealth they accumulate to their university in the form of donations while they live and as bequest when they die. In addition, if the alumni do not devote time and money to raising children and following the dictates of their religions, they will be able to accumulate a great deal more money to give. The function of institution evolution is strengthening the organization at all costs, therefore elimination of families and religion from the lives of students is an effect of institution evolution.

The term alma mater (meaning nourishing mother) demonstrates this competition with the family. The fear mongering on campus concerning the future overpopulation of the world when, in fact, almost all industrialized nations have negative population growth falsely discourages alumni from having children. The United States has not had replacement reproduction for the last 30 years, yet those who are college educated have much fewer offspring than the average American does.

I once filled out a distinguished alumnus application, and the second, seemly irrelevant, question was "How many children do you have?" This award is given to encourage alumni to contribute to the alma mater, so the university does not want to waste it on someone with offspring.

I do not mean to imply that most professors on campus purposely discourage students from having children to help the university obtain money from the alumni. I am simply stating that the universities that happen to discourage procreation become the most influential because they get more money. With a larger college-educated segment in society, the philosophies from these "best universities" now tend to dominate society, and this indoctrination of the most educable regarding offspring has become one of the most damaging to our society.

America is evolving into an uneducable society, which will destroy the universities in the long-term. The good-student genes are being depleted from the gene pool. Essentially all of our most educable people receive higher education, which then greatly cripples their ability to have offspring. Thus, the educable are going extinct, with grave consequences for America and extremely grave consequences for these families. It also contributes to one of the biggest problems with the apparent decline in the quality of public schools: the children of the most educable are few, and most of them are not sent to public school.

To rationalize this devastation to society, "BEEism" (BEEism is a name I chose for the set of Beliefs produced by the Evolution of higher Education. A BEE is a believer.) preaches that the ability to become intelligence and the ability to learn are bestowed on all equally and conveniently ignores the genetic influence on these abilities. This false tenet appears to be protected by another false concept that race genes are practically the same as intelligence genes, making it taboo, because it is deemed racist, to talk about intelligence being hereditary.

Elementary science, however, indicates that people, to a large degree, inherit their ability to learn the same way they inherit their race but these two characteristics are produced by different genes, just as height and eye color are produced by different genes. Thus, the two characteristics are not genetically linked to each other and no race has a monopoly on intelligence or the ability to learn. Nonetheless, both of these independent traits, to a large degree, are inherited.

BEEism insists that Darwinism be taught in school, while choosing to ignore that our ability to learn depends, in large part, on our genes. The inconsistency of this position is so obvious as to be laughable. Institution evolution is, once again, the culprit.

The false dogma of equal educability became part of BEEism to prevent Darwinism from undermining the effective sterilization of the alumni. Otherwise, the educable would realize their responsibility to reproduce and prevent this immoral depletion of our ability-to-learn genes from the gene pool. They would have more children, which would decrease the money going to the alma mater. The reason BEEs emotionally insist that Darwinism be taught in schools even while ignoring any genetic effect on educability is that Darwinism is naively thought to undermine belief in God and the advanced religions, another big competitor for alumni money.

BEEism rails against religion. Any belief in God is ridiculed on campus. In the past, the existence of God was discussed on campus, but that does not happen much today. Now the secular campus philosophy declares that religion is bad. This philosophy helps these universities in their competition with religions for money from alumni. Even if alumni do not have children, they might leave their estates to their churches instead of the university. If the alumni can be both sterilized by the belief that their children would be bad for the world *and* converted to the religion of BEEism, they will be very helpful in making their university the richest and, thereby, the best.

Unfortunately, the fallout from this particular form of institutional evolution is the removal of God from public life, which makes maintaining a democracy very difficult. (See the Appendix.) Without God as the alpha, the indisputable one who makes the rules, anarchy results and humans will compete to become the ruler or the ruling class. The animal within the human wants to rule and thinks the subgroup to which he or she belongs is superior and should rightfully rule. Without God, this animal instinct leads to war and murder between these groups and even within them. Believing God is the master of all humans, and in God's eyes, we are all of equal value, equal brothers and sisters, keeps us respectful of each other. This respect is an essential ingredient to a peaceful democracy.

Today, the biggest threats to our freedom are from groups that consider themselves the elite (such as the rich, the media elite, the Ivy League elite, some religions, and the political leadership) or consider themselves oppressed (such as the blacks, the gays, some religions, and the feminists). All of these groups are strongly influenced, directly or indirectly, by BEEism, and it is therefore tremendously important to recognize its destructive teachings. When this country was founded, it was recognized that, for democracy to survive, the members of society must believe that all people are "created equal with certain inalienable rights". Now we must recognize that, unless they have a deep and real belief in a Creator who values all human life, it is extremely difficult for humans to grasp the concept of equal worth. Without God, the animalistic instinct of elitism dominates people's thinking, and the oppression or even extermination of inferiors by ruling supremacists is logical. Supremacists caused the Holocaust.

BEEism teaches that physical force should not be used to resolve differences or enforce rules. Clearly, if only the power of the pen is allowed and the power of the sword is outlawed, then the highly educated will have the most power and wealth, maximizing the power and wealth of the institution of higher education. Thus, BEEs are against the military, the police, and private gun ownership.

BEEism also teaches that corporal punishment for children is extremely immoral. Convincing students that their parents' disciplining was egregious is a step toward breaking their family bonds, undermining their parents' values, and converting students to BEEism. Removing this very powerful tool from child rearing makes the students lose confidence in their ability to rear children if they cannot rear them the way they were raised, for they realize the loss of this powerful tool makes a difficult job nearly impossible. Thus students will be less likely to have children and, therefore, more likely to give their alma mater more money after they graduate. Again, the beliefs of BEEism have evolved to make the alma mater richer in the short-term.

The evolution of the institution of higher education has stimulated the feminist movement. Clearly, teaching hatred of men, as well as the false concept that men and women are the same except for their environment, has high value in extracting money from alumni. It creates women who either will be very unsuccessful in marriage or will not get married at all. They probably will not raise children and may even choose a lesbian lifestyle. They become sterilized females, perfect workers for their alma maters, just as sterilized females are the worker bees for beehives. The effect is extremely family extinguishing.

Feminists and BEEs strongly support Title IX and women's athletics. Inducing women to be devoted to sport reduces their femininity. Women athletes sometime even stop menstruating, becoming not just virtually sterilized but physically sterilized. Competitive athletics tend to produce strong, aggressive, competitive, and sterilized women, perfect for their alma maters. Of course, some exercise is important for good health but the level required for highly competitive or professional women's sports is family extinguishing.

The hate training being taught in women's study courses has caused tremendous damage to marriage, to children, to men, and most of all to women. Previously, women were the center of the family, providing most of the physical and emotional support for the rest of the family and receiving in return vast amounts of love, recognition, and gratitude from all concerned. The man's job was to supply the basic resources for the family, but woman had the most important job of using those resources to care for everybody. Women had the right to be proud of the successes of their children and husbands because her nurturing made those successes possible. However, today's women are taught that only their own personal monetary success is of value. This is absurd. They are taught this because it is, indeed, all that is valuable to their alma maters. (This also benefits their employers' institutions, which will be covered under business institutions.) What is worse, these ideas are taught to all women through media that is controlled by educated men and women.

Educational institution evolution has weakened the female support needed by children and men while overburdening women with the sense of need for a moneymaking career. The resultant destruction of the family and marriage continues to greatly decrease the number of educable offspring. The decrease in offspring of our best and brightest women combined with robbing children of their mothers' nurturing is taking a toll on the number of quality children being produced, not to mention the happiness of women and children. In a couple of generations, we will not have enough highly educable people to support a modern technical society that is highly educated. The greatest injustice is the extinction of some of our best families.

Institution evolution also explains why higher education is one of the strongest advocates of the gay lifestyle. If an alumnus is converted to BEEism and is also turned into a homosexual, he or she becomes the ideal worker bee for the university. Homosexuals are not likely to have children, their families will likely disown them (no chance of leaving money to the nieces or nephews), and few religions will accept them. If no time or money will go to offspring or a church, they will probably accumulate much more wealth than the average person, with much of it going back to the alma mater.

The University of Illinois is one of the top universities in agriculture. Robert Henry Allerton, whose lifetime male companion graduated from the U of I, gave a great deal of land and resources to the U of I, helping it to become one of the best. This is a classic example of how the acceptance of the gay lifestyle helps institutions of higher education, causing this acceptance to become part of the BEE creed that is being forced on society. This encouragement of homosexuality has had and will continue to have important negative effects on our society, such as the supporting of the feminist movement and the elimination of gay genes.

To avoid getting into the genetic-versus-environmental reasons for a person being gay, let us assume that both have an effect. In our present society, where it is acceptable for people to live in a homosexual relationship, the reproductive rate of gay genes is greatly reduced. Thus, the gene pool is being depleted of the gay genes. Most people wouldn't think so, but this is a great loss. Many of our great scientists are men with female tendencies and women with male tendencies. Some of our best artists and actors are gay. In fact, the influence on Hollywood by gays has added powerful fuel to this extremely damaging movement.

It is postulated that one form of human body becomes either male or female with only minor physical changes. The body chemistry of this one form is not perfect for either the male brain or the female brain, and compromises are made during the body's development using different hormones to allow either gender to exist in basically the same body design. Therefore, brains of people who have tendencies toward the middle, between male and female, seem to function better in the human body than those of people who have strongly male (jocks) or strongly female (bimbos) characteristics. Assuming these "transitional" types of people tend to be gay, it will be a great loss of brainpower from the gene pool if condoning the gay lifestyle eliminates reproduction. People with gay tendencies offer a different view of the world and have talents that are needed by our society. It is a mistake to allow these genes to be depleted. Because of this loss to society and the extinction of the family lines of homosexuals, no one should accept homosexual relationships as moral.

Lesbians suffer the most from a traditional society where men bring home the resources and women use them to nurture the family. Lesbians do not have a high position in a traditional society were women derive their power and status from the accomplishments of the men and children who depend on them and appreciate them. Without a man or children, the lesbian is left powerless. Therefore, the almost complete control of our governments by BEEs has created a high demand, via affirmative action, for women in jobs normally done by men. Since these are the jobs that only lesbian (as opposed to heterosexual) women really want, this situation creates great advantages for lesbian women and corresponding disadvantages for normal men and women.

Widespread BEEism has led to the co-mingling of men and women in the workplace. This places a strain on families and marriages and decreases the amount of work done. Contact with the opposite sex at work may lead to the straying of sexual loyalty that can certainly destroy families directly; however, even just having a close working relationship with members of the opposite sex may cause dissatisfaction with one's spouse. Marriages are weakened by outside sexual competition, but they can be strengthened when both of the partners find each other more interesting and enjoyable because they have interacted with only members of their own sex at work. The natural and healthy situation is for men to work with men and women to work with women. This is especially true since men and women both tend to communicate better with members of their own sex, which increases the efficiency of their work. Many men are particularly distracted by the presence of women, while women often feel intimidated by men. Thus, the co-mingling causes added stress both at home and at work, leading to less work getting done and much less happiness. Once again, the gay men and women benefit from co-mingling, while normal men and women, who are producing our next generation of children, suffer. Thus, co-mingling of men and women in the workplace is a family–extinguishing practice.

Until relatively recently, only slave males and females where expected to work side by side at the same tasks. We are all becoming slaves to big government and big business. Once we recognize this co-mingling in the work place as a perverse consequence of institution evolution, this unhappy situation can be corrected. See Chapter 6 for a couple of solutions.

Now, spouses who choose to stay home are being taught by BEEism through the media to question "the fairness" of a system that requires them to "do all the work" at home, causing them to overburden their working spouse with nurturing responsibilities. This puts the working spouse of a family at a disadvantage in competing with gays and other effectively sterilized workers for the highest paying positions. Thus, the ones most likely to give their wealth to the alma mater will make the most money in the workplace. Before this family-extinguishing value was implanted, having a stay-at-home nurturing spouse gave the working spouse a much-deserved advantage in the workplace, because he/she would have more time and energy for work. The stay-at-home, nurturing spouse did everything possible to support the working spouse in bringing home resources for the family, including doing most of the household chores. This traditional role helped the family survive as long as the working spouse spent as much time with the family as possible, but not to the point of taking away his/her advantage at work.

Along with the gay rights and feminism perversions, the pro-abortion philosophy has sprung from the institution evolution of higher education. Abortion kills the major competitor for alumni money—children—and is a strike against most religions, the other main competition for alumni estates, while it maintains the financial productivity of female alumni. It further discourages the rearing of children by directly lowering the status of the unborn and pregnancy and by less directly lowering the status of children and motherhood. Therefore, BEEism advocates abortion.

I have a difficult time with the abortion issue. It is the legal murder of one human by another. To allow this in society is a major blow against the concept that God has given all humans the right to life, liberty, and the pursuit of happiness. It is all too easy to rationalize that some humans are not really human so it is moral to kill or enslave them. This was the rationalization behind slavery. Once you cave-in to the idea that some humans have more basic rights than others, you undermine the basic principles of the American experiment and are well on the way to destroying our system of government.

On one hand, this pro-abortion type of supremacist thinking led to the Holocaust. (Many more humans have been killed in America due to abortion than were killed by the Nazis during the Holocaust.) On the other hand, children grow from their parents and are the parents' responsibility. They carry the parents' genes and are almost an extension of the parents, and they are most definitely members of the family unit that grows from the parents. Therefore, we might allow the family an abortion or even infanticide to remove a member, just like we allow the removal of a disease-damaged limb from an individual's body. In some cases, the survival of the family may depend on ending a pregnancy, in which case, the baby's genetic survival through its family may depend on its death. For example, the drain of the family resources required to take care of an invalid child could prevent the birth of productive children and therefore extinguish the family. Finally, from a Darwinian point of view, it might be a good idea to allow the children of murders and other societal undesirables (a category within which pro-lifers might include pro-abortionists) to be aborted or even murdered. And, by extension, since birth control is readily available, it may be a mistake to protect the children of people who are irresponsible or stupid enough to get pregnant when they do not want a baby.

Abortion is a difficult moral issue because once an unwanted pregnancy is started there is no moral solution. Of course, if it were a purely moral issue then much more energy should be spent on preventing unwanted pregnancy and much less on debating the issue. Unfortunately, for the abortion industry it is a money issue. In the mechanism of unrecognized and uncontrolled institution evolution, morality always loses to money: thus we have legalized abortion.

It is preposterous that the U.S. Supreme Court is so unchecked, corrupt, and arrogant as to take upon itself the legislation of this difficult issue instead of allowing it to be settled by the elected officials at the state and local levels as provided by the Constitution. If the decisions were made locally, more people would live under abortion laws with which they agree; and with 50 states seeking solutions, a much better compromise would be found than one settled on by a handful of politically-motivated, BEE judges. The Roe v. Wade legislation has caused the abortion issue to unnecessarily divide the country. (See Section 1.1 of Chapter 3 for more about Federal courts.)

Even those who do not believe that all humans are valuable to God should understand that, if we allow a woman the God-like choice to take the life of another, even her own child, we strike a blow at the Constitution. We must be vigilant against the strong human tendency to claim fundamental superiority over other humans. Elitism and the denial of another's human dignity are extremely strong human weaknesses and perhaps the greatest causes of human suffering. We must not pander to this evil by allowing abortion on a whim as we do today.

It is absurd that, in our present society, a woman can freely elect to have an abortion, even if she is married, even if the baby is her husband's, and even if the father wants the child. Women can ignore their responsibility for their own fertility, commit the sex act unprotected, and conceive a child, and then abdicate responsibility to bear the child, take care of the child, or produce the next generation; however, the man, who more often than not has less control of his sex drive, cannot abdicate his responsibility to support the child if one is born. This is completely unjust. If a woman is allowed to have an abortion without her husband's consent, then the husband should be able to abdicate his responsibility to support his child without the woman's consent.

Men are driven to provide for women both by a need for female company and by the pleasure of sex. Men are, by nature, essentially slaves to the women they find attractive and are rewarded genetically for this devotion with offspring. It is a crime against nature that women can command this devotion without allowing its natural result. Allowing abortion or even birth control to be exclusively the woman's decision gives too much power to women.

Women are now given preferential treatment for college admission, even though well over half of all college freshmen are women, because they make the decision concerning having children. A BEE female has the will and the power not to have children. A BEE male does not have the power or probably the will to prevent a fertile wife from producing children. Thus, women are the preferred student because they are less likely to have children. In addition, women tend to outlive men and spouses usually bequeath most of their wealth to their surviving spouse. Thus, the sterilized women who marry will have fewer choices for bequeathing all those assets and tend to give the jointly earned money to their universities when they die. Between sterilization, hate training, total reproduction rights, and female longevity, the alma maters of female alumni should recover large amounts of money.

The unjust abuse of the power of total reproduction rights is probably the cause of much of our domestic violence. The high profile cases of the Blake and Peterson double murders, where husbands kill their pregnant wives, are probably examples of this injustice leading to violence. Suppose a married man who does not want more children has a vasectomy and then his wife gets pregnant. It is totally unjust that, if his wife refuses an abortion, he will have to support that child to adulthood. Desperate, unjust situations like this cause some fools to see murder as the only solution. Remember, to find peace we must seek justice; that is, injustice begets violence. Our present unjust laws concerning domestic relations contribute to domestic violence.

Abortion might be legal and constitutional if it is done with due process. There certainly is no due process in our present system, where one person is judge, jury, and in some cases executioner. Due process might include following these four rules: 1) Both parents of the fetus must be involved in the decision, and the parents of minors must be involved in the case of minors having an abortion. 2) The parties involved must be educated so they can make a well-informed choice. 3) The fetus must not have reached a stage where it could be viable outside the womb. 4) It must be shown that having the child will cause severe damage to the family.

Both parents should be involved in the abortion decision, even though the baby is in the woman's body, because women should always have the right to avoid pregnancy. (In the case of rape, some procedure should be carried out immediately after the rape to assure no pregnancy occurs.) The "work" of carrying a child during the first nine months is a small fraction of the total effort required to raise a child. Properly rearing a child represents a large commitment from both parents, and the child is the offspring of both parents, so the decision to abort has to be a joint decision. In the case of a pregnant minor, the parents of the minor have responsibility for the care of both the minor and the baby and need to be involved in all decisions for the process to be just. A woman should be required to identify the father of her baby before she can receives any help, from any institution, with having and raising the child. The father needs to be known not just to obtain his help with rearing the child, but to assure that everyone knows his or her genetic parents to prevent future accidental incest—an inherent danger in the present adoption system.

In order to make the correct decision, the parties involved need to know the form or stage of development of the fetus they are considering killing. When making any decision of this importance people need to know exactly what they are doing. The problems with giving babies up for adoption are mostly fabricated by the abortion industry. Specifically, a mother who suffers remorse at giving up her baby and goes berserk trying to get it back will suffer the same remorse—maybe greater and definitely irreversible—toward having had an abortion once she realizes how established her pregnancy was (the stage of development of the fetus) and that interfering with an established pregnancy is tantamount to murder.

Logically, we cannot allow the abortion of viable babies unless we allow parents to also kill their minor children at any age, and I think it is fairly clear we do not want that. It is absurd that we spend hundreds of thousands of dollars to save premature babies, while at the same time we allow unborn babies of the same age to be killed. It is also absurd that abandoning to death a day-old baby is considered a major crime while aborting a baby the day before it would have been born is legal. Finally, it is extremely unfair to healthcare workers who are trained to save lives to ask them to kill a baby that could be saved, and of course it would be stupid to take a baby and then save it if it could go full term. Thus, viable babies must be allowed to finish their gestations.

The possibility that having the child would cause more damage than good for the family's survival has to be a major consideration in this decision. The net damage, however, must be severe enough to justify such an egregious act as abortion. Just as we allow solders to die for our country we might allow the unborn to die as long as it truly for the survival of that family.

Unfortunately, any legal procedure that allows abortion will be used by corrupt pro-abortions judges and lawyers to approve any abortion requested. Thus, almost any process that allows abortion, in practice, amounts to abortion on demand and must be illegal.

And then there is divorce. In the most simplistic scenarios, people should have the right to choose how to spend the money they earn. If a woman divorces a man and takes his children, since the decision to have the children (to use or not use birth control or have an abortion) is deemed by society to be solely the woman's, the man should not be forced to support them. A man should not be forced to pay for his wife's home when he does not have the comfort of her support and he should not have to pay for the support of his children when he does not have the joy of participating fully in their lives. Most men would voluntarily support their children after a divorce, but no one should be allowed to force them or to dictate what constitutes adequate support. The U. S. Constitution forbids this indentured servitude and much of the domestic violence that occurs during and after divorce would probably be eliminated if this injustice were stopped. Presently, men are required to support their ex-wives and children—often with the man living in poverty—because the government does not want to pay these "dependents" welfare. This is another example of judges conveniently ignoring the Constitution. Since society as a whole makes it so easy to divorce, society, not the abandoned spouse, should pay the cost of caring for the victims of divorce, which are the children.

Since women can use modern science to control their reproduction, men should be allowed to use modern science to assure that the children he is supporting are indeed his own. A man should never be forced to support a child he did not conceive, unless he agreed to his wife being fertilized by another's sperm. Genetic testing of babies should be mandatory at birth. Men would then know their children are really theirs, even if some question of their wives faithfulness arises. In addition, adultery, which is very damaging to the family and children, would be further discouraged. It is unjust and genetically extinguishing to the man's family line to force him to use his resources to support a child that is not his.

The question that begs asking is "How can educated people believe the philosophies advanced by BEEism?" Part of the answer is that "educated" simply means those who are educable and have passed through the higher-education institution. It does not mean "thinking" or "intelligent", and it certainly doesn't mean "wise". Educable means you can rapidly understand and apply new concepts; however, critically judging the value or truth of concepts requires deeper thinking and intelligence or wisdom. These characteristics can be distracting and may even make a person less educable because he or she will not accept at face value the information he or she is being force-fed. (Einstein was a poor student.) Thus, the educated are just as susceptible to fallacious concepts as anyone else. Another part of the answer concerns the students that are not very gifted. They are particularly vulnerable since they are fully occupied with passing individual courses to obtain a degree and have no extra time or energy for resisting the constant exposure to BEEism. However, the strongest force for broad acceptance of BEEism is educational elitism. After four or more years of very hard work furthering their education, people want to think they are fundamentally better than the un- or undereducated. To many, accepting the beliefs of BEEism is part of demonstrating that one is educated and therefore superior. They lie to themselves as well as others, "I understand these principles and you don't," when, if they really understood the principles, they would "understand" that they're just wrong.

Indeed, some of the beliefs are so perverse that they do separate the educated from normal people. Since many have lost their true belief in God, they are powerless to resist the appeal of following educational elitism and its BEEism doctrines. This dogma has lead to the atrocity of murdering tens of millions of unborn children and to the weakening of the family unit and religion. It is causing the genocide of the American population, especially the educable. It is causing a rapid demise of the American culture of freedom and dignity for all people. The saddest part is the loss of the individual family lines that are being extinguished.

From ancient history to the present, elitist ruling classes, such as the Babylonians, Romans, Nazis, and Communists, have inflict great suffering on humans that they deem inferior. The world wars were the result of elitists trying to take over the world: the Nazi European supremacists, the Japanese Far East supremacists, and the Communist global supremacist. The common traits of these supremacists included highly developed discipline, following leadership without question, and an apparent disregard for personal freedom.

All supremacists feel they should naturally be in control of other humans because they are the chosen people. They follow their rules and are, therefore, not very creative. Their desire and ability to follow their leaders in lockstep and the immoral alliance formed through the illusion of their superiority is the source of their power. Elitists falsely believe they should lead humankind because of their superior skills and intelligence or because it is their God-given position, and they are always a threat to the freedom of humanity. They speak of inferiors as niggers, queers, homophobes, protected classes, rednecks, uneducated, teenagers, minorities, newly rich (new money), infidels, and gentiles. We must learn to recognize and control this most barbaric and damaging instinct. All humans must be allowed full dignity.

BEEism is closely related to Communism. Communism is a total system for human existence that professes a political system, a system of economics, and a belief system of moral values. BEEism is so close to the belief system of moral values of Communism that Communism probably grew out of BEEism. In the former Soviet Union, college professors were the most respected and powerful professionals.

Many campuses have become environments of righteous enforcement of BEEism. Before the Vietnam War, only intellectual arguments carried much weight on campus. During the war, the campuses turned into battlegrounds against the war. In the end, emotion and perceived righteousness led the movement, and intellectual discussion was suppressed. The university should teach people *how* to think, not *what* to think. We must get over Vietnam and replace the emotional righteousness on campus with intelligent intellectual discussion. The only punishment for wrong or indefensible statements should be the loss of respect caused by the revelation that the statements are wrong and indefensible.

The campuses have not yet recovered, and they continue to righteously enforce BEEism while suppressing dissension and intelligent discussion. An intelligent discussion would reveal that the population explosion, for industrialized and postindustrial countries, is a myth. We would quickly see that voluntary birth control by the brightest and most educable segment of our population is self-defeating. Although highly intelligent educated people can contribute to society during their lifetimes by working, it is more important that they also contribute to society forever by having many intelligent, educable children. The more talented they are, the more important it is that they have children. Obviously, our best and brightest should be having the greatest number of children.

Voluntary birth control also eliminates the genes that cause people to volunteer and will become less effective as the volunteer genes disappear. Volunteers are very important for a happy society. We should stop selectively breeding out volunteerism by ending the encouragement of voluntary birth control, especially since we do not have a population growth problem. The U.S. population is growing because of immigration, not because of reproduction. We are presently brain-draining the world and, through birth control, selectively performing "voluntary" genocide on the intelligence after it arrives. What we are doing to mankind is unbelievably immoral and it is, ironically, contributing to a world-population explosion.

It is a fact that, presently, industrialized countries have a negative population growth, while the pre-industrial third world still has "explosive" population growth. Thus, industrialization of the third world is the best way to achieve zero or perhaps negative world population growth. It is the intelligent and educable of those countries who will lead the industrialization of the third world. Thus, our present system of stealing these people from their homelands prevents the industrialization of the third world, exacerbating the world population explosion.

The solution to population growth is for industrialized nations to have children, but only enough to replace themselves. Instead of lending third-world countries money and giving population-growing medicines and technologies to them, post-industrialized nations should be financing high-quality, practical educational systems in third-world nations and teaching them their obligations to help their home countries. Of course, it is moral to help with the health concerns of third-world nations, but the concurrent harvesting by industrialized nations of the third world's brightest citizens, those who would be most likely to help them achieve industrialization, is extremely immoral and is actually fueling the world's population growth.

In summary, the evolution of higher education has produced an outrageously immoral belief system that I have called BEEism. It is Godless and actually anti-religion and encourages abortion.

It teaches hatred of all non-BEE males and that men and women are identical except for environmental factors and a few different body parts. It encourages the gay lifestyle and feminism. It teaches that reproduction is immoral and ignores that intelligence and the ability to learn is genetic, while inconsistently teaching Darwinism. It teaches educational elitism and pity for minorities, who are silently viewed as inferior and in need of affirmative action. It teaches that corporal punishment is immoral. These "politically correct" beliefs have so permeated the power structure of this country that speaking out against them can illicit severe punishment. These BEE values are extremely family extinguishing and, therefore, anti-family.

Higher education's genocide of the educable can be controlled. Care must be taken because the present rules do encourage the training of productive members of society. (The alumni must make money before they can give it back to the university.) Parents are the big losers due to the effective sterilization of their children. The first step in turning this around is for people to understand what is going on and why. Parents must educate their children about the concepts presented here before sending them to college. Parents must investigate the domestic success of the school's graduates before they send their children to a college. They should find out the marriage rate, the divorce rate, and the average number of children per alumnus and avoid sending their children to colleges with poor results in these areas. Colleges and universities should be required to supply this information.

Alumni contributions to their alma maters should not be tax deductible, and tuition should be tax deductible as a learning-to-do-business expense. This would give the parents more influence in higher education. Some fraction of the income tax that children pay should be returned to their parents, as a reward for making their children productive citizens. This would make parents more interested in the outcome of the children's education, allowing successful colleges to charge more tuition. Colleges and universities (and all institutions, for that matter) should be taxed the same as any business. All money they receive should be treated as income and taxed at the flat rate as described in Section 1.2. In addition to eliminating the deduction for charitable contributions we should start taxing endowments and endowment income. [Receiving a tax deduction for money given to certain institutions but having to pay taxes on money given to our family members—and additional taxes if that money is more than a specific amount per family member per year—shows how absurdly powerful and abusive (to our families) our institutions have become.] The extra tax money received by the government should be used in funding higher education in such a way that universities receive more money when the alumni have children. This will cause higher education to evolve so that it instills pro-family survival values instead of the anti-family values it instills today.

The government should progressively forgive education loans as graduates have children. The government should give money, with no strings attached—bonuses, if you will—to universities based on the reproduction rate of the alumni. We should not change the amount of money the universities receive, but change the way they receive it so the fertility rate of graduates becomes at least as high as the general population. If all else fails, government funding for education should be decreased in proportion to the donations and endowments the university receives. Even more drastic, alumni should not be allowed to contribute to their alma mater until after they have at least two children.

As in the United Kingdom, we should require competency tests upon graduation. America's present Graduate Record Exam or something more extensive should be required at graduation. The government should give money to the universities based on the number of students they graduate who attain certain levels of performance on this competency test. The amount of money could be adjusted to compensate for the loss of favorable tax treatment of alumni donations, keeping the same or more money flowing to the universities.

Changing the rules in these ways would not only combat family-extinguishing values it would also improve higher education. The universities now often think of the students as future alumni and tend to dumb-down education so all future alumni will feel good toward the university and return contributions. The changes proposed will make the families the customers, and the universities will respond with better education.

The rules on how universities obtain money must be changed so they will evolve away from consuming most of the best and brightest genes of mankind through BEE indoctrination. Millions of years of struggling for survival by the alumni's ancestors is being thrown away just to make the alma mater rich. Thousands of years of religious culture is being abandoned for the benefit of the alma mater. We must stop this. When the universities are evolved to be family supportive, it should be much easier to get taxpayers' support and reverse the present trend of decreased state support of higher education.

The *US News and World Report* must stop using the amount of alumni contributions as one of its rating criterion, or it should recognize those amounts as correlation with the effective sterilization rate, because the use of this factor as a positive rating criterion exacerbates the problem. If they want grandchildren, parents should avoid sending their children to places with high alumni contributions.

The people in higher education, for the most part, are very moral, good people who want to do what is right. They also learn very quickly, and institution evolution is an extremely powerful force leading them to do and teach what is best for the institution rather than what is best for families. We must change the rules so that what brings in the most money to the universities also supports survival of the students' families.

✳ ✳ ✳

2. The Extinguishing Impact of Psychiatry

Applying the concept of institution evolution to the psychiatric profession leads to interesting results. The leading psychiatrists are the ones that make the most money. In order to maximize their incomes, psychiatrists need to make patients feel better at the end of each visit so they will come back and also so they will recommend their doctors to friends and relatives and increase the business. In order to insure that people come back, behaviors and philosophies of life are encouraged that will keep people mentally ill. These patients are also advised in child rearing such that their children will soon need a psychiatrist. The effects are extremely damaging to the family. Not only are they taking the family wealth they are teaching family-extinguishing values. Remember, psychiatrists are not purposely doing this, but the ones that happen to do this end up making the most money and building large successful clinics, thus becoming the most influential.

It is true that when people first visit psychiatrists they are usually in very serious mental pain. The first goal of the psychiatrist is to help patients feel better so they can cope. The quickest way to achieve this is, unfortunately, for the psychiatrist and patient to blame others for the patient's problems, and there is a real tendency for psychiatrists to encourage patients to do this. Blaming others who are close to the patient, but who are not present to defend themselves, is a natural tendency, so parents and spouses are the prime candidates. For the psychiatrist this is particularly nice, because this method results in patients distancing themselves from people with whom they would normally be very close and from whom they would normally receive help and support. This loss of support makes patients more dependent on their psychiatrists for all social needs. Thus patients will spend more time, which equals money, with their psychiatrists, and the institution will thrive.

A great deal of damage to families and marriages occurs because of this tendency to blame those close to the patient. In addition, the patient is not helped to develop the life skills needed to prevent problems in the future. While still feeling mental pain, the patient would be more willing to adopt new and better life skills, and moving quickly into learning new life skills would be much more efficient and less damaging to the patient's life. However, this method is not used because taking responsibility for one's own feelings and actions is harder and less pleasant for the patient and psychiatrist, which means the patient may stop attending necessary sessions or may not need to attend as many sessions. In light of the psychiatrist's need to blame someone else to keep the patient happy and coming back, the following simple rule should be followed: if your child or spouse starts seeing a psychiatrist, you had better accompany him or her, unless you want to be blamed for everything and your family to be destroyed. You might want to apply that rule to parents and siblings also, if keeping your family close matters to you.

One indication of monetary influence within the profession is the stand of leading psychiatrists against corporal punishment. When rearing children, some type of punishment is essential to prevent undesirable behavior. Adults can use either physical or mental punishment. In either case, those administering the punishment must use restraint and intelligence to avoid severe damage. Psychiatrists prefer mental punishment because they make more money when extensive mental damage occurs.

Corporal punishment, for children, is far superior to mental punishment for several reasons. It is an extremely clear communication of a parent's disapproval, and this disapproval causes the pain. The message speaks to a very basic level that cannot be reached with language. It should not cause significant physical pain or harm, and a few simple rules can prevent damage. Corporal punishment can be administered very quickly at the instant of bad behavior, giving it the greatest corrective value, and even more important, it stops very quickly. It causes little mental damage because it is not administered face to face. It is also much easier to detect excessive physical punishment and take corrective action. Overall, this form of correction does not waste time, is more effective, and is less likely to produce lasting emotional damage.

Mental punishment requires a level of interpersonal skill and verbal skill to express the reason it is being administered and the expected result of the punishment without diminishing the self-respect of the child (or even spouse) and without resorting to name-calling. It also requires the mental skill to determine what non-corporal punishment fits the "crime". The result must maintain the authority of the giver and the respect of the receiver and not be abused to cause mental anguish or resentment on the part of the receiver. Many (perhaps most) people do not have the patience, perception, cleverness, and verbal skills required for the safe and effective use of mental punishment. When corporal punishment is disallowed, their children are either spoiled from the lack of discipline or abused from a bungled attempt at mental punishment.

Unfortunately, since the opinions of leading psychiatrists are respected and BEEism is also against it, the Federal Government, controlled by BEEs, has essentially outlawed corporal punishment in the United States. People often lose their children if they try to raise them with proper discipline. The Federal Government has accomplished this indirectly through bribery, by requiring states to pass overly restrictive laws as a condition for receiving welfare assistance. The highly educable and their few children have strong verbal communication skills and are more docile; therefore, they have less need of powerful corporal punishment for control and discipline. The docile nature they display comes in part from an extreme fear of pain, making corporal discipline appear horrific to them. Those who are less educable, however, especially males, understand actions much better than words. Disallowing action as discipline is disallowing less educable people the right to rear their children, especially their boys, correctly.

Outlawing physical punishment, while allowing mental punishment, is a direct consequence of the evolution of the psychiatric profession and higher education. It has led to mental damage and lack of self-control in today's children. It is especially damaging to male children since they often do not respond to mental punishment before grave—sometimes permanent—damage has been done, while, on the other hand, harmless corporal punishment would have been very effective. The resultant spoiled or abused children are the ones who often commit violent crimes, much to the surprise of the permissive or abusive adults in their lives. These parents and teachers think they are doing the right things. Unfortunately, however, they are listening to the ignorance of institution evolution.

Physical affection and physical disapproval are essential elements in a healthy father-child relationship. Removing that makes it very difficult for a father to be both loved and respected by his children. Having both love and respect for his father is a key element in the son wanting to become a father and in a daughter wanting a husband. Thus, eliminating either of these from the relationship discourages children from producing grandchildren and is a family-extinguishing value. The male haters that do not want the fathers involved with their children are strongly against corporal punishment.

One way to evolve psychiatry away from being ineffective or actually causing problems and toward quicker, better, long-term solutions for the patients is to simply change the way psychiatrists are paid. The psychiatrist should have a fixed fee for diagnosing a patient's problem. Depending on the nature of the illness and the disposition of the patient, the psychiatrist should then make an offer to "cure" the patient for a fixed amount. With contract cost curing instead of open-ended by-the-hour curing, return customers become liabilities, so cures will become quicker, more complete, and more beneficial to the family. The contract could include prevention of negative side effects on the family. Thus, the profession would evolve into a more beneficial institution.

3. The Evolution of the National Government

1.1 Evolution to Big Government

The basic human need to be important and take care of associates puts continual pressure on the growth of government. Our founding fathers were well aware of the tendency for government to grow and become oppressive. They carefully crafted a document that spelled out exactly which powers the Federal Government would have, with all the remaining power being kept by the states. In addition, the Federal Government was organized with a balance of powers between the Legislative, Executive, and Judicial branches. It was limited in its ability to raise money. The state governments appointed the Senators. In addition, a new President and new members of Congress would be periodically elected. In principle, the executive branch can be changed every four year, the House of Representatives can be changed every two years, and the Senate every six. Unfortunately, the Federal Government has been able to overcome these obstacles, and it continues to take more and more wealth, power, and freedom from the families it was designed to support.

In 1913, two amendments to the Constitution removed major restrictions on the growth of the Federal Government's power. One was the 17th Amendment, which requires the U.S. Senators to be elected at large from the states instead of being chosen by the state legislators. Before this amendment, Senators were powerful leaders of their state governments and as such they identified with that institution. They were responsible to the state government and represented it in Congress, rather than representing the people of the state directly. In the short term, this amendment immediately lowered the power of the state governments, since they lost Senatorial control of the laws passed by the Federal Government. In the long term, this greatly increased the power of the Federal Government because state governments lost control over the appointment of Supreme Court Justices.

Previously, the Senators' approval of the Supreme Court appointments insured that the powers of the state governments would not be usurped by the national government. A court that belonged to both would judge the competition of the two governments for power using the Constitution as the rulebook. Now the Justices have no ties to the state governments and belong entirely to the national government. Therefore, based on the institutions-try-to-grow rule, the Court "interprets" the Constitution to increase the power of the Federal Government. The Constitution is now just a hindrance, and the challenge is to technically defeat it to allow progress toward total Federal Government rule and tyranny. The balance of power between the state governments and the national government, which had kept both in check, is now lost. For example, this Court allows the logically unconstitutional practice of the Federal Government bribing the states to give up their powers by offering Federal financial assistance to states if they follow specific rules set up by the Federal Government. The Supreme Court has also allowed extremely liberal use of the power of the Federal Government to regulate interstate commerce.

In summary, before the 17th Amendment was passed, the state governments checked the national government's control of the Federal Court system through their state-appointed Senators' approval of these appointments. Now both the Senators and the President derive their power through the national government, and the Federal justice system, by the rules of institution evolution, serves to maximize the power and money of the Federal Government.

One solution is for state legislatures or governors to approve appointments to the Supreme Court instead of the Senate. That the state governments should have no control over the appointment of Supreme Court Justices is logically absurd. Unfortunately, it will be very difficult to reverse this blunder since constitutional amendments must start with Congress and institutions rarely voluntarily give up power. However, elected bodies sometimes relinquish institutional power if the survival of the individual elected official depends on pleasing the voters and obtaining funding for election campaigns.

The state legislators did so in approving the popular election of U.S. Senators, fearing the demise of their own popular re-election. This tells us the correction requires the mass education of voters and a grass-roots movement.

Judges who serve on the benches of the state courts are usually elected, but the President appoints, with Senate approval, those who serve on the benches of Federal courts. The election of judges allows a certain influence by campaign contributions on the courts; however, since the judges must periodically win the people's vote and since campaign contributions are public information, they cannot rule obviously in favor of a big campaign contributor. This combination of a need for campaign money and a need for the people's votes seems to produce reasonably good results in electing judges as well as legislators. The appeals process also helps to keep judges honest. On the other hand, Federal judges are appointed and receive their positions for life as political favors. Very often, the President or one or more senators will approve an appointment in return for favorable treatment on some legislation. This system is political and corrupt. It serves the political needs of the Federal Government, but it does not serve the people, nor does it pursue truth or justice.

The Rodney King case is a classic example of the operation of the corrupt system. In this case, a bystander videotaped the LAPD arrest of a black man, Rodney King. The news media did the standard tabloid hype of the incident and showed only selected parts of the tape to give the impression to the untrained eye that the police were being overly abusive to the criminal King. However, viewing the entire tape shows that King never submitted to arrest and was aggressively fighting with the police from the beginning to the very end, until he was forcibly restrained.

The police were trying to get King to submit to arrest by harmlessly hitting him with glancing blows of their nightsticks, to no avail. They are trained how to do this, and the fact that King sustained no serious police-inflicted injuries proves they did a good job. The entire tape shows that the police acted with professional constraint. However, they did hit him with sticks, so the media edited the tape to produce the maximum amount of hate in the black community, which had the desired effect of causing a riot—desired because it sold many ads for TV news. Because of the riot and hype, the involved police officers were tried in state court; however, they were found innocent, which a viewing of the entire videotape proved they were.

The Federal Government, on the other hand, sensed that political benefits could be accrued by finding the police guilty. They therefore arrested the police for "violating the civil rights" of King. The Federal court did not allow the tape to be shown to the jury, who unjustly convicted the police officers due to this withholding of evidence. This is a classic example of the Federal court system doing what is politically advisable, with no interest in truth or justice.

The trial of Timothy McVeigh, in the Oklahoma City bombing, is extremely suspicious, where both the judge and McVeigh's appointed attorney had worked for Nixon. The politically correct result was more important than truth or justice. Under the Clinton administration, the rapid loss of interest in John Doe #2 indicates that the government wanted to conceal the identity of a person who initially was considered likely to have masterminded this bombing. The attempted hasty execution of McVeigh further strengthens this "conspiracy theory." McVeigh and Nickels did not have the talent and resources to carry out the bombing acting alone, and there is evidence the Federal Bureau of Investigations (FBI) knew something was going to happen.

Under the succeeding Bush administration, new documents were found that had been "accidentally" (read: illegally) withheld from McVeigh's defense lawyers. These papers contained a great deal of information about John Doe #2. Bush delayed the execution for one month (probably to find out if there was anything in the incident he could use against the opposition) before he allowed the execution. Even under Bush, however, one senses the strong impression that the truth is probably not being told, nor is justice being served.

Finally, the recent Federal court ruling that the Food and Drug Administration (FDA) cannot regulate tobacco is patently absurd. This ruling obviously helps to remove the government's responsibility in the damage to health caused by tobacco. The ruling was handed down to strengthen the Federal Government's legal case against the tobacco industry for illegally causing medical expenses for the government. The government has subsidized tobacco growing and enjoys enormous amounts of tax revenue on the sale of tobacco products, and logic would lead one to assume the government is therefore guilty of collusion. However, by taking the position that it was helpless to control tobacco, the government is now able to get even more money from the industry based on healthcare costs. The smokers end up paying all of these effective taxes, with none of the money returning to them for extra health care because they actually spend less on health care throughout their short lives than longer-living non-smokers. The system has evolved to the point that there is no justice or truth . . . just politics and the procurement of the greatest amount of money and power possible for the government. The money comes directly or indirectly from American families, making their survival more difficult.

The present system of Federal judges appointed and approved by Federal politicians is flawed and needs to be changed. Lower court judges should run for office in the Federal Court districts. States need to have veto power over Supreme Court appointments. Because the Federal system is so flawed, the state justice systems should be required to investigate all deaths in the state, especially when someone dies in connection with the actions of the Federal Government. For instance, the Texas Rangers got much closer to the truth about Waco than did the FBI. There should have been an independent state investigation of the Oklahoma City bombing before the FBI destroyed the evidence. Congressional Representatives should automatically investigate any deaths in their districts in which any Federal Government entity was directly or indirectly involved.

The other amendment passed in 1913 that greatly increased the power of the Federal Government was the 16th amendment, which allowed the income tax. This is a family-extinguishing tax because it is placed directly on the wage earners that support most families. The income tax gives the Federal Government a large source of income that it uses to bribe the states and the citizenry to allow it to control the country. It does this directly by putting stipulations on essentially all the money it spends, from scientific research to road construction, and indirectly by allowing tax deductions or tax credits for activities it wants to support. This use of bribery by the Federal Government to usurp the states' powers is contrary to the Constitution and is only allowed because the Supreme Court is entirely controlled by the Federal Government.

The Executive Branch has also given up power by signing into law the Federal Civil Service Act. The idea behind this law was to give the government continuity from one President to the next and to prevent the appointment of incompetent people as a result of political favors. However, the real result was to make it very difficult for the President to fire low-level bureaucrats. These low-level career bureaucrats do not answer to anyone. They spend their funds to maximize their impact on Congress so they will get more money. If Congress tries to restrict their activity, they redefine the language used in laws in such a way that they can continue pursuing their own personal agendas. As long as Congress continues to fund them, these little fiefdoms continue, answering to the people only weakly through Congress.

The most dangerous of these bureaucracies are those that gather information and are licensed to kill people, such as the Central Intelligence Agency (CIA) and the FBI. It has become very clear that the President has little power over the FBI. President Clinton was using the Waco blunder against the FBI while the FBI was using the Los Alamos/Lee disaster against Clinton and the Justice Department. Clearly, if the President were in charge of the FBI, such a conflict could not arise. President John F. Kennedy might not have been murdered if he had been in charge of the FBI, the CIA, and the United States Secret Service. Many people believe that these organizations were involved in the assassination and certainly in the cover-up.

The Warren commission on the Kennedy assassination is another example where the most beneficial political solution was all that mattered.

The Civil Service Act prevents elections in this country from being "bloodless revolutions" as the founding fathers had designed them. Much of the power within the government does not change hands after an election because it is held in the bureaucracies of civil servants who serve only job security. Thus, the Civil Service takes power from the people and our families. The solution to this problem is to only allow the lowest level government employees to be civil servants. Anyone who is a supervisor, who recommends or does the hiring and firing, or who recommends or approves pay raises should be appointed. These appointees would still only have to represent around 10% of all government employees, so continuity between presidents would be maintained, but the newly elected President would be able to make policy and philosophical changes through his appointees. More important, people loyal to the President would control the government.

For example, J. Edgar Hoover had considerable loyalty to Johnson and Nixon but hated Kennedy. Kennedy had defeated both Johnson and Nixon to become President, and after JFK was taken out of the way, both men had their turns at being President. Although Hoover's position was appointed, he and his loyal institution had so much damaging information about the Kennedys that JFK could not fire him.

Presently, the very highest-level positions are appointed. However, the most powerful positions, like the heads of the FBI and CIA, should have strictly limited terms so that J. Edgar Hoover-like disasters cannot be repeated. The killing of Kennedy and his replacement by Johnson not only showed that the government is out of control, it dramatically changed the course of American history. Although Kennedy did have advisors in Vietnam, he had begun to withdraw them because South Vietnam did not have a government worth supporting [A&E television "The Men Who Killed Kennedy: The Witnesses"];

however, Johnson reversed the decision and led the U.S. to actually begin fighting the Vietnam War. Johnson also instituted "The Great Society." Both of these acts by Johnson had devastating effects on our society, ranging from the warped evolution of higher education and political thinking to the abuse of the poor via welfare.

The people are supposed to control the Federal Government through the election of the legislature and the President. The elected officials must please the people to retain their offices, and, perhaps more important, they must attract money from the people and businesses to finance the propaganda campaigns needed to convince people to vote for them.

The fact that the people elect the government gives control to the people, were it should be. The fact that the officials need money in order to be elected is also good because it is important that the wealth of the country be productive so we can all be better off. Giving money some control of the government helps to assure this. However, there must be balanced control to prevent enslavement by the government and/or big money. If the people's money had no control, we would all be poor, as in Communist countries.

At the time of the industrial revolution, big money controlled the government, which in turn helped big money to enslave the people. Presently, the power of the government is too high, and it is growing rapidly. A large amount of money is spent on election campaigns because people and businesses know it is worth the investment to have influence on the way the government spends its massive revenues. The best way to limit the power of the government is to lower the amount of money available for it to spend. Our families should keep this money and taxes should be lowered.

Unfortunately, the combination of the Civil Service system and the needs of elected officials for campaign money has led to the control of most regulatory agencies by the industries they are supposed to regulate. Together, the agency and the industry it is supposed to regulate become a legal monopoly. That is, the agencies organize their industries for maximum profit and to eliminate competition, making the cost to the family much higher.

Because of Civil Service, these regulatory agencies only answer to Congress through its control of their budgets. The industry that an agency is supposed to regulate contributes to the campaign funds of key congressional representatives who set the regulatory agency's budget. Thus, the regulatory agency is controlled by the industry it regulates.

Until the Reagan administration, the Federal Aeronautics Administration (FAA) was a classic example of an agency controlled by the industry it is supposed to regulate. In fact, it still is, but the FAA's powers were decreased so that it is not as strong a monopoly. Of course, we all know how the cost of flying decreased with deregulation.

The FDA is so controlled by the industry it supposedly regulates that it routinely makes it illegal for people to put the truth on their products. For example, a food product cannot say that no genetically altered plants or animals are used in making the food, even when that statement is true. In another case, it is illegal to truthfully say that the cows producing milk were not given synthetic hormones. The FDA "knows", with very little testing, that certain genetically altered or synthetic products are safe and uses the elitist concept of protecting the public from its own ignorance about the supposed safety of the products to justify preventing ordinary citizens from making their own choices based on the truth. Who benefits from this behavior? Industries trying to sell genetically altered and synthetic products, of course, and those who invest in those companies. And why would the FDA care? Big Businesses pump big bucks into the pockets of those who decide how the FDA will be run. In fact, the big money spent by the industry it is supposed to regulate is turning the FDA against the people in more and more cases. This is costly to families that need low-cost high-quality food and drugs.

The concept that regulatory agencies tend to be controlled by the industry they regulate also applies to the FBI and the CIA. It is well known that J. Edgar Hoover was controlled by organized crime (which threatened to expose his cross-dressing behavior). He refused to recognize organized crime, calling it a conspiracy theory, until it had grown into an extremely powerful organization that may still control the agency. CIA reporting is part of the motivation for building up our military; therefore, the military industry would benefit the most by controlling the CIA through Congress. The "bad intelligence" from the CIA that was used as an excuse to go into Iraq is strong evidence that the military industry controls the CIA.

Agencies such as the military, which are set up to control organizations outside the country, do not end up being controlled by the outside organizations for two reasons. First, it is illegal for foreigners to contribute to political campaigns (no money can be obtained from the outside organization, so its proliferation is not a concern of the regulating agency). Second, our entire government would be disbanded if we lost to a foreign power (the institution would be committing suicide if it allowed a foreign power to dominate it). Institution evolution rejects this possibility.

Fortunately, the naïve establishment of the military works because as the institution grows it does a better job. The military may spend much more money than is necessary and it may exaggerate the threats to our security to preserve itself, but our military system has worked well or our government would not have lasted over 200 years. The people in the military are well aware that they stand to lose the most if they do not do a good job; however, it remains to be seen where the evolution of a peacetime professional military will lead. The power and influence of the military has led to an overly powerful peacetime military.

Unfortunately, the constitution was not designed for a powerful peacetime national military. It was designed around each state having its own militia. When Congress declares war, the militias are to be organized together, with the President as Commander in Chief. There was no peacetime national military under the President. Logically, the President would not be Commander in Chief during peacetime, and certainly not with by far the most powerful military in the World, because our forefathers knew that in this situation the President would use the military for his own political ambitions. Specifically, the biggest threat to the President would be the opposition political party, so he would use the military primarily for political advantage. For instance, President Clinton would initiate some military action in an attempt to divert public attention from his sexual relations with his intern. President Bush, however, has taken this abuse to a new level with the war in Iraq.

Clearly, President Bush must be a political genus to have become President with his very poor public speaking abilities. He, as most Presidents, is driven almost entirely by doing what it takes to win politically. He puts up trial balloons and watches the political response. If it looks like an action will help him politically he does it. This is almost certainly the primary reason he attacked Iraq. He could see from the response to the suggestion of this war that it would divide the Democratic Party. The Democratic Party has very strong pacifist and Zionist elements and the war is perfect for dividing and weakening the Democrats, so President Bush went to war. Indeed, the war put the Democratic Party in disarray and they lost the 2002 and 2004 elections after the war was started. They may have won the 2006 election because the Zionists finally realized, after Israel's defeat by Hezbollah in Lebanon, that turning Iraq over to the Shiites is more dangerous, for Israel, than having it ruled by Saddam Hussein. The party then became more or less united against the war in Iraq.

The first way to stop this very immoral behavior is to cut the size of the military so we cannot start a war without some risk to our own security. We need to break-up the media so that there might be some intelligent voice of opposition heard as we prepare for a really ill-advised war. In our present situation, somebody should have had the power to demand to see the non-existent data that showed Iraq had weapons of mass destruction.

We need to limit the Commander-and-Chief power of the President in peacetime. For example, a joint bipartisan House and Senate committee could be set up to approve all peacetime military action. This committee would have an independent intelligence agency to gather information. Requirements for membership to this committee would be the same as to be President in addition to being elected to Congress. People with dual citizenship or guaranteed citizenship in another country could not serve. The intent of the constitution is that the President can only take military action with Congress's approval. Since our peacetime military needs rapid response ability, a small independently informed committee of Congress should be sufficient for quick approval of limited military action. The Committee would have no military appropriations responsibilities nor could the members sit on such committees. In addition, the National Guard should answer to the Governor of their state unless Congress declares war and the president should not be allowed to call up the National Guard or Reserves unless Congress declares war.

We spend more on our military than the next 20 countries combined spend on theirs. This is way too much. The cost of maintaining this large military put us at a disadvantage economically that will lead to the loss of our world leadership. The government should let families keep more of their income while decreasing the size of our military. This would strengthen the families and strengthen our economy. Having such a large military advantage leads to the irresponsible use of its power, such as the unnecessary and ill-advised takeover of Iraq. If our military had been weaker, we would have spent more time garnering support from other countries before we attacked. This would have prevented the act from appearing so irresponsible, and maybe it would not have done so much damage to our image throughout the world. Maybe the war would not have happened.

The biggest danger from an overly powerful professional military is that, because of its increased influence throughout the country, it could overthrow the government, leaving us with a military dictatorship. Having separate military branches helps to prevent a military takeover because the branches would have to act together; however, the likelihood of a military overthrow has never been greater than it is today. The present professional (read mercenary) military is much more dangerous than a drafted one because the soldiers are more loyal to the military when it is their career and the only life they know. A large number of the men in the military are part of the unhappy mateless subclass that is prone to revolt against the ruling elite, as discussed in the Appendix.

There are many reasons for these men to have this oppressed and valueless feeling:

1. We are now enlisting people without a high school education, clearly society's dropouts.
2. BEEism, with its control of the mainstream media, has been hate mongering against males for the entire life of the present typical enlistee, making young men feel valueless. In the form of "situation comedies" and other fare, the media, marginalizes or even minimalizes the intelligence and respectability of fathers and males in general.
3. Men are discriminated against and treated unjustly in the workplace, especially in government employment.
4. Men are treated unjustly in laws concerning domestic relations.
5. The impact of the sterilization propaganda of higher education has trickled down to the K-12 level, teaching that people have no value and only overpopulate the earth.
6. BEE teachers indoctrinate boys that they are inferior to girls in every way and that males have no value.
7. The constant hammering of children with environmental concerns has made young people feel that humans are evil and the bane of the earth.
8. The wholesale murder of millions of their generation through legalized abortion further lowers the value of lives in the assessment of this generation.

9. The false praise given to them as children in an attempt to reverse the debilitating effects of institution evolution on their egos has removed young people's respect for authority. False praise undermines the ability of legitimate praise for real accomplishments to raise one's estimation of self or others.
10. As children, many of these young men were raised with a lack of discipline. Failure to discipline is the sincerest expression of low expectations and devaluation.
11. Many males have suffered mental damage from attempts at discipline through mental punishment.
12. Children are not being taught that they are valuable to God.

Most of what we are doing wrong is policy developed by the evolution of higher education, psychiatry, and big business enforced by the Federal Government. In the perverse process of rearing our girls to be soldiers we are rearing our boys to be terrorists. A society that is producing neither good soldiers nor good mothers will not last for very long. We do not have much time to prevent the demise of our entire society. These problems have already caused the demise of many families. The atrocities a military coup would inflict on this country could be horrific, especially since all other governments of the world would be powerless to stop it. It is extremely important that all citizens be armed with military-quality weapons to lower this threat.

Our forefathers attached the second amendment, the right to bear arms, to the Constitution so that the ultimate power would rest with the people and not with the government. The elitists in the government would like to usurp this power and end the American experiment. We need to remember that guns had been outlawed in almost all other parts of the totalitarian world at the time of the American Revolution, and democracy took over in the one area where gun ownership was legal.

Democracy is not the natural human social structure, and we must be diligent or it will be lost. After winning two world wars, the influence of our country has stimulated the spread of Democracy. Unfortunately, a government will not respect an unarmed population. The reason we have less freedom and less respect from the government than ever before is because the citizens are less armed relative to the government than they ever have been. People only have as much freedom as they can defend. It is simply a matter of power begetting or suppressing freedom. Control is in the hands of those who have the power. Ultimately, power is firepower, and that must remain in the hands of the citizens. When guns are outlawed in the USA, the world will very quickly return to its normal state of totalitarianism. Since there are no new frontiers where the citizens can accidentally become armed, Democracy will be dead forever. It is naive to think otherwise.

Registration (of gun owners) is the first step toward annihilation. If you do not believe this, ask the surviving European Jews. If you think our government would never annihilate people because they have guns, ask the survivors of Ruby Ridge or Waco. If you think our government will respect people who have inferior firepower, ask Elian Gonzalez's U.S. relatives.

The government, not the people, needs a reduction in firepower. It should be illegal for the government to use weapons on U.S. citizens that are illegal for law-abiding citizens to buy and own. This law would help to prevent the elitist mentality of swat teams. Such a rule may also help prevent the police from accidentally shooting other police and innocent citizens.

In the American experiment, everyone must have equal status. This prevents oppression by elitists and the resultant hate of oppressors. We are all equal lieutenants under God. A clear signature of lieutenants in any society is that they have power and are armed. Outlawing guns from the general population would remove most of the population from lieutenant status and transfer them to the oppressed subclass, ruled by the elitist armed government. Outlawing guns would undermine the ability of families to defend themselves. Thus, it would be a direct removal of power from the family, further weakening its position and value in society.

The anti-gun movement appeals to the animalistic instinct of elitism by arguing that gun owners are low-class, irresponsible people, unlike the elitist, the police, and the government. They make the false argument that; somehow, gun ownership by good citizens causes violent crime. In fact, law-abiding gun owners are like free mini-police, and right-to-carry laws have decreased crime with almost no abuse by these gun owners. It turns out that armed citizens have a better track record of shooting the criminal than the police because they are at the scene and witness the crime. Police usually arrive at the scene after the crime is committed and sometimes misjudge who committed it and punish the wrong person. Outlawing guns in the United Kingdom and Australia caused an increase in crime, and the crime rate is still growing.

An enslaved subclass is not armed. An armed person is not enslaved. The police bureaucracy will grow if people are not allowed to protect themselves. The way to stop drive-by shootings and rare mass murders is to raise all people with self-discipline and morals and a firm recognition that they and we are extremely valuable lieutenants of God. Only members of a mateless oppressed subclass are desperate enough to shoot somebody to prove their own value.

For each person desperate enough to shoot someone else, there are tens of thousands who have been ruined by our oppressive, passive, Godless environment and are ready to join a revolt against this system that has relegated them to such a low-level position. We must fix the environment, not outlaw the tool (guns). Outlawing guns would exacerbate the problem, possibly leading to violent revolution due to the resultant massive increase in the oppressed underclass.

Finally, would-be shooters are being offered millions of dollars worth of free publicity by the news media to commit horrific crimes. This encouragement is extremely immoral. Therefore, publishing the name or picture of a murderer, especially a mass murderer, should be considered as immoral as publishing child pornography. In both cases, people are being destroyed to sell press. The faces and names of the suicide pilots of the 9-11-01 attack are rarely seen in the media, showing that the media knows that free exposure encourages the behavior. Unlike school shootings and other mass murders, the 9-11 attack was so horrific, on New York the home of much of the media, that the media does not want a repeat.

1.2 Guaranteed Income, Flat Tax

Our present tax structure, Social Security, and retirement plans are family-extinguishing. The Social Security System taxes one generation to take care of previous generations, which is unfair to the people that raise children because their children are being taxed to take care of the childless freeloaders. It is silly to think that a whole generation can save for retirement and use their money for retirement without the need for children to take care of them. In the end, somebody has to do the work to take care of them, and if nobody had children then there would be no young people to care for the elderly. What is really unfair in our system is that the people who spent their money and energy to raise children have less money to buy retirement care from the next generation. This disadvantage to the reproducers is one reason that industrialized, capitalistic countries with retirement plans have negative population growth and many families in these countries have been extinguished. This family-extinguishing disadvantage is greatest for the best and brightest families because college costs make raising children even more costly. This disadvantage must be removed by changing the tax structure, the retirement systems, and the cost of raising children so that people have at least enough children to replace and take care of themselves.

The present situation of allowing favorable tax treatment for money saved in retirement accounts is family-extinguishing. This gives preferential treatment to money that people turn over to bankers or employers on the hope that the bankers or employers will take care of them in old age. (Good luck with that.) This leaves less wealth to their children, but then the bankers and businesses have better lobbyists than the families. This tax loophole, like most of them, is family-extinguishing. Families should receive the same tax treatment to keep the money so their children are in a better position to take care of their aged parents. It is a question of who controls the wealth. The family-strengthening approach of children taking care of their own parents and inheriting their parents' wealth is heavily taxed. If this were not so, more families would be accumulating more in order to be able to take care of themselves throughout their generations. Retirement accounts also receive special treatment in being protected from lawsuits. Investing for one's care in old age should be encouraged, but preferential tax treatment for money turned over to bankers and business instead of being kept by the family and/or invested in the children is family–extinguishing and should be discontinued.

Social Security and retirement systems weaken the family in another very important way. Not only does it discourage reproduction but it also removes the motivation to raise children *properly*. If children are not going to take care of you in your old age and are gone in any material way after they become adults then there is little reason to spend the large amount of effort required to raise them to be productive, loving, and respectful. If the wealth is kept in the family then the children need to be taught to respect and to take care of their parents in old age. The family is much stronger because it develops an understanding of mutual nurturing. The parents take care of young children and the children take care of parents in old age. This traditional system engenders much more mutual respect and love between parents and children. Thus, disrespect for parents and the old and the failure to raise our children properly all stem, in part, from the expectation that the government, rather than the family, should take care of old people. This needs to change.

The Chinese religion of venerating your parents and ancestors has helped them to survive for many thousands of years. (Unfortunately the present communist, oppressive government in China is enforcing family extinction by making laws such as allowing only one child per couple.) While it is one of largest and most successful religions in the world, Chinese traditional religion is almost totally ignored in our society because governments, universities, and industry want people to devote all their energy and give all their wealth to the government, their alma-mater, and big business, and these institutions control our thinking.

The animalistic instinct of people to want more resources and to increase the size of their tribe is the underlying cause of the growth of government and of government bureaucracies. That people support the group of people they know is an endearing quality, and most bureaucrats are good people. However, when the legislature sets up and funds a bureaucracy to solve a problem, the bureaucracy soon realizes that once they solve the problem, they will be disbanded, but the worse the problem becomes, the more money the bureaucracy receives. Thus, as we well know, government involvement often makes things worse. The Department of Agriculture and The Department of Education are examples of such problem-exacerbating bureaucracies in the Federal Government.

Many of the inefficiencies in governments would be solved if the legislatures would be very careful to make sure that the bureaucracy grows when it lessens the problem and shrinks when its problem gets worse. This may seem strange, but it is the only way to make bureaucracies successful. A simple method to achieve this is to list all things we want the bureaucracy to make happen and list all the things it is to prevent, and then increase or decrease its budget depending on its success. The function of the elected officials would be to make the list and assign the reward and/or punishment for each item on the list. The beauty of this method is that we would then know very clearly the purpose of the bureaucracy. In addition, the list with the quantitative rewards and/or punishments would make a very clear quantitative framework for debating the goals and the funding of the bureaucracy. This method would make it very difficult for lobbyists to use regulatory agencies to monopolize an industry.

As an example, consider the FAA. We want air travel to be inexpensive, which might be measured by the amount of air travel. We also want to prevent accidents, which might be measured in accidental deaths due to air travel. If we give the FAA, say, a dollar per 1000 passenger miles traveled in the USA and subtract from its budget, say, $300,000 for every accidental death, the FAA would make travel cheaper and still keep it safe. We would simply need to make sure that increasing airline profits is not on the FAA's list.

The road-building Department of Transportation bureaucracy, which gets its money from gasoline taxes, is one example of a successful bureaucracy. The more roads that are built, the more gasoline is used, and the more money the bureaucracy gets. This bureaucracy very effectively built the freeway system in the U.S. Unfortunately, there is a glitch. Once gridlock occurs, building more roads and, consequently, freeing up traffic would actually decrease gasoline consumption because creeping, stop-and-go traffic consumes much more gasoline to move people to and from work than smooth, speed-limited flow. In these instances, the bureaucracy would rather support public transportation because the bureaucracy will grow if public transportation increases, but it will shrink if it builds more roads decreasing the consumption of gasoline. Therefore, once traffic jamming starts, much of the bureaucracy's funding goes into pro-public-transportation propaganda and little or none into road building that helps the gridlock. Another reason the government wants to keep traffic congested is that people will accept higher taxes if they believe the lie that something will be done about traffic congestion if they pay more.

One solution to this freezing of road construction might be an equation for Department of Transportation funding that gives less money to the bureaucracy when traffic jams occur. The tax money not given to transportation could be given to some other bureaucracy, such as education, which would "help" the transportation department measure jamming and would determine the amount of jamming penalty. The goal is to base the size and budget of the road bureaucracy on the amount of traffic it *moves* on the roads and remove the money it makes from jamming. Public transportation and road construction should be in a completely separate bureaucracies with rules on how each can grow as it moves more people. If the two are together, road building will be stopped to force the funding of public transportation.

The biggest, and fastest growing, bureaucracy of all is our current tax and welfare system. It involves several bureaucracies and is anti-family. It encourages the breakup of the family by requiring the father to leave a poor family before they can get welfare. It taxes a family that stays together more than one that is split up. It pays daycare expenses for a mother that leaves her children in order to work outside the home but pays nothing to a poor mother that stays home and takes care of her children while her husband works.

The Department of Health and Human Services (DHHS) is a good example of a typical bureaucracy that is straightforwardly set up to solve a problem. This welfare bureaucracy receives more money when there is more poverty; therefore, its self-preserving policies must increase poverty. Consequently, policies have been put in place so that once a person is on welfare it is almost impossible to get off.

The marginal tax for working (tax on next dollar earned) is often higher than 100%, crushing any incentive to get a job. In many cases, the only way for these people to get ahead is to have more children, which creates more temporary cash flow but, in the end, more poverty and, of course, a bigger welfare bureaucracy. Healthcare and Social Security problems are handled the same basic way. All of these bureaucracies are large and growing while not solving the problems.

The solution is a different tax/welfare system that replaces our income tax, welfare, healthcare, and Social Security systems. This method would take advantage of a bureaucracy's tendency to grow and would accomplish a much fairer, simpler, and more efficient redistribution of wealth than our present system. This simple system will decrease the number of single-parent homes, decrease poverty, decrease crime, decrease drug abuse, decrease the animosity between the rich and the poor, decrease the hate between blacks and whites, bring men and women closer together, decrease government and hatred of the Federal Government, help stop the decline of the middle class, and slow the growth of healthcare costs. It would increase the health, freedom, and wealth of families.

This system would provide a Guaranteed (minimum) Income and a Flat Tax (GIFT) for every voting-age US citizen and every college student who is a US citizen. The IRS, through employers, would administer the GIFT system. In this system, the tax rate is the same for everyone. A tax credit would be given to individuals through employers who would be required to provide acceptable medical coverage as determined by Congress. The tax credit would subsidize the company payroll by much more then the cost of the required medical coverage. State governments could act as "employers" for the unemployed (transferring the guaranteed income from the Federal Government to the people and providing medical coverage). The total welfare cost to the state might remain about the same since the state would only have to pay for health care. The Universities could do this for unemployed students. The company of the employed spouse could do this for an unemployed spouse. Corporations and all institutions would have the same tax rate as individuals but no tax credits. (However, dividends paid to stockholders would be considered corporation expenses for tax purpose.) There would be no loopholes, and the only adjustments to income would involve capital gains and interest income *in excess of inflation*, which would be considered income, and interest paid *in excess of inflation*, which would be deductible from your income. Finally, to enforce mutual nurturing and encourage parents to raise their children as productive members of society, some fraction (say 25%) of the income tax a child pays would be returned to the parents for as long as the parents live. This would give parents a financial return on the investment of raising their children properly. The exact fraction could be determined by the amount needed to prevent the present extinction of the highly educable.

This system takes advantage of the way bureaucracies work. In order to solve the poverty problem, we must give it to a bureaucracy that will receive more money with the elimination of poverty. Therefore, having the IRS administer a flat tax with a tax credit independent of income is the correct solution since the IRS receives more money as poverty is decreased. The idea is not new; the present income tax has an "earned income tax credit" which gives a tax credit to low-income workers. The new system, however, would be simpler and provides more help for low-income workers. Getting such a system passed by Congress, however, will be very difficult because it will mean killing the powerful welfare bureaucracy and decreasing the size of the government in general.

Figure 1 shows a graph of tax versus income. In the GIFT system, the government gives low-income people extra income. The proposed system does not subsidize divorce and the destruction of families, as our present system does. In the Figure, the total taxes and total income are plotted for two parents with two children, including social security tax paid by the employer and workers (in 2000). The two working parents are assumed to have identical incomes.

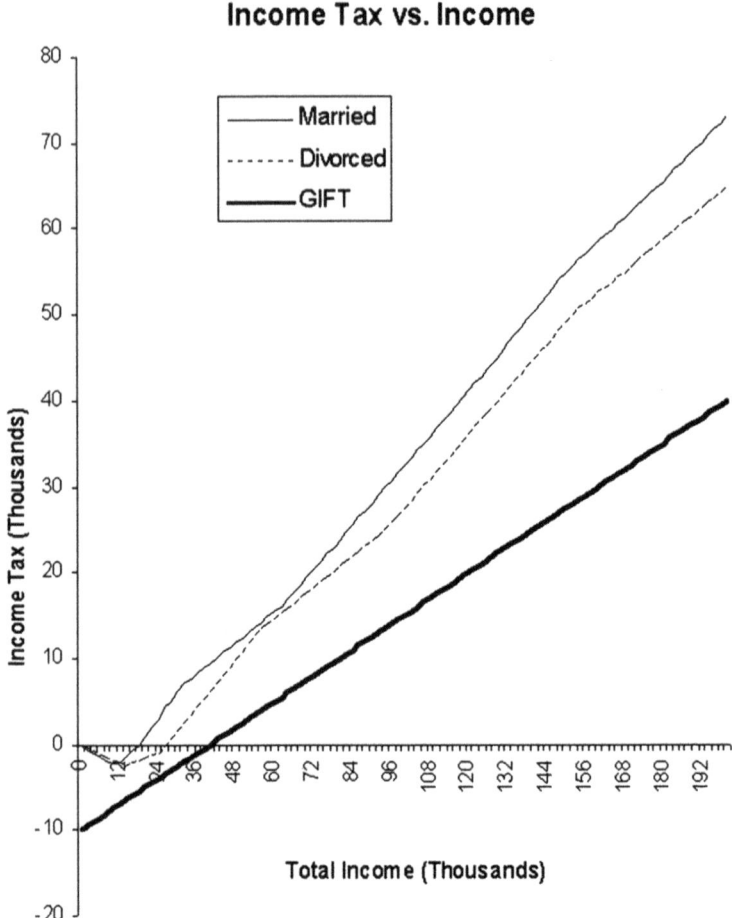

Figure 1. Income tax verses income for a presently married and divorced family and the proposed guaranteed income flat tax (GIFT). The guaranteed income is $5000 per person and the tax is 25%.

For the present tax system, there are two curves: one for married parents and one for divorced. Notice the taxes are lower for the divorced parents. This is what is called the marriage penalty. Clearly, it is anti-family and anti-children because it has financial incentives for divorce. The curves include Social Security and Medicare taxes paid by the company and the individuals. It is interesting that our present system nearly equals a 39% flat tax with a 3% marriage penalty and a $5000 guaranteed income per person. In this present system, the lower income part is filled in with welfare payments, which are not shown on the plot.

There is only one curve for the proposed tax system. The tax rate is lower (25%) because there are no loopholes, and the government will cost less with no welfare system and a less complex tax system. Our present tax structure is regressive because the rich have more loopholes, like paying taxes on only 15% of their capital gains income, deductions for charitable donations, and no social security tax on high income. If anything, taxes should be progressive, as is the GIFT system.

One problem with the GIFT system is that it does not provide care for the excess children already born to the poor because of the incentives of the present system. Instead of giving tax credits, deductions, food stamps, or cash to poor parents for the support of their children, the Federal Government should start a free meals program for *all* children, to be administered under the Department of Agriculture through the schools and daycare centers. Breakfast and a midday meal on school days and a mid-morning meal on free days should be provided without charge.

As much as I dislike having the government in our lives, proper nutrition is essential for good learning and growth. In the past, the Federal Government heavily subsidized the free lunch program, and I think it worked well. The free meals for all children approach has the following advantages: it gives equal benefits to all children, it provides proper nutrition for all children, and it saves working parents the time and effort required to feed their children breakfast. The best part is that it prevents the starvation of poor children without financially rewarding the irresponsible adults who have more children than they can afford.

The GIFT system would reduce government and the hatred of government. The whole tax/welfare system would be reduced mainly to two numbers: the tax credit (amount of wealth redistribution) and the tax rate (amount of government). This would enable all voters to understand the debate and vote wisely. One reason people hate and fear the government is that they do not understand the tax laws and consider them unfair, as they indeed are. This system would replace all of the health and human services part of the Federal Government and replace family-extinguishing Social Security.

This system is fair because it gives the same tax rate, the same marginal tax, and the same tax credit to everyone. Every adult U.S. citizen owns an equal share of the infrastructure of the United States and has equal responsibility in defending this country against outside aggressors. As a return on this ownership and responsibility, each adult citizen deserves a minimum survival amount of income. This is especially true for people whose ancestors were forced to come here or were living here before Columbus came. The conservatives should consider the guaranteed income as necessary for the removal of a much greater evil, the welfare system. The tax credit would provide a survival only level of income. Retired people that did not raise children to care for them and/or did not saved for retirement do not deserve more than this.

A major unfair situation that exists under the present system is the medical care received by welfare recipients. Many taxpayers with low-end jobs are paying taxes that provide Medicaid benefits to others, while these taxpayers receive no healthcare benefits themselves. This type of injustice makes people hate the government and hate blacks, who are often perceived as the largest class of welfare recipients in this country. The new system eliminates this unfairness and this hatred.

Businesses benefit from this system because the Federal Government will subsidize employees' salaries if employers provide healthcare benefits. This salary subsidy would prevent small employers from paying employees in cash and illegally not paying taxes to the

IRS. For low-end jobs (most of which do not now have healthcare), the healthcare costs will be a large portion of the employers' labor costs, and their incentive will be great to work very hard at keeping this cost down while still providing enough healthcare to receive the subsidy. This will ripple through the industry and slow the growth of healthcare costs.

The new system would allow people to work their way out of poverty and encourage families to stay together by giving financial value to unemployed men and women. It would remove the present financial incentive that encourages divorce, fatherless homes, large poor families, and teenage unwed mothers. Since everyone gets the same tax credit, there would be no stigma associated with it as there is with welfare. Presently, we are creating a mateless subclass, because women cannot get welfare if their men are around and being on welfare is not an honorable situation. Eliminating these effects should lead to less crime and fewer drug problems among the poor.

With the largest marginal tax of anybody in the country; no wonder people on welfare have a feeling of hopelessness. The inner-city gang/crime problem is a natural response to a system that takes away boys' fathers and takes away men's wives and children. The males in this situation are presently the mateless subclass that naturally forms gangs and fights the overly oppressive elite. (See Appendix) To expect anything other than anti-establishment gangs in a mateless subclass is naïve. The present system demands too much moral character from the men in this situation.

The time has come to free the poor families from the welfare system and allow them to solve their own problems. The proposed tax system is progressive, yet everyone has the same marginal tax and tax credit. This allows people to seek meaningful, even if low-wage, work without losing benefits—to make a contribution to society while working out of poverty. It provides a minimal retirement and healthcare plan for everyone as well as support for college students.

The GIFT system would eliminate tax deductions for contributions to charitable and non-profit organizations. Allowing such tax deductions while taxing money set-aside for children is anti-family. A better system is to have a lower rate overall, with all money received by all individuals and all institutions taxed at the same low rate, including gifts, inheritance, and capital gains. It is unfair to allow tax deductions for the rich when they donate money to non-profit organizations. They do this for recognition and enhanced respect from the community. They get full value for their donation and should not get a tax deduction as well. Many of the non-profit behemoths created by this system, like universities, have led the charge against the family as discussed in Chapter 1. All institutions should pay taxes on their net income, even if it is put into an endowment. All institutions should also have to pay property tax. An overall lower rate is more valuable than the benefits from loopholes that mostly help the rich, the tax lawyers, and the tax accountants.

Donations to charitable foundations often cost the government much more than the donors. To see how this happens lets assume the tax rate on the donor is 40% and that he donates greatly appreciated stock. If he gives $100 to his foundation he can control the charitable use of that money and deduct it from his income he saves the tax of $40 which he can spend as he pleases. If he just sold the stock he would get $60 to spend as he pleases. Thus, for the $100 he spends through his foundation he only loses $20 with the government contributing $80. This has to stop!!

The GIFT system should have an adjustment in the tax rate and the tax credit for individuals based on the number of children they support. The benefit per child would need to decrease after the third child is born. A combination of lowering the overall tax rate and making the tax credit larger when people have children can be used to achieve two targets: 1) control of the overall population growth and 2) control of the relative number of children of the rich versus the poor. Making the tax rate lower encourages the rich to have more children while giving a larger tax credit encourages the poor. We can easily stop the present higher reproduction rate of the poor, and we can control population growth. Along with this, we need to stop our present net immigration. This will allow the survival of both rich and poor families. Our present family-extinguishing result of negative population growth of American families and more than making up for it with immigration needs to be corrected. In addition, allowing the immigration of large numbers of lowly paid workers into the US is anti-family because it lowers the standard of living for working people, especially young people because raising a family is more difficult when there are more people competing for resources, from jobs to schools to real estate.

Presently, the poor have more children than the rich, which is one reason the wealth is becoming concentrated to a lower percentage of the population. If the rich had more children than the poor, the wealth would become less concentrated. Presumably, the people who are paid the most for their work have more of the talents that society needs today. Thus, we should be increasing our gene pool with these talents, and these people certainly have more resources to properly educate their children. Therefore, it would be better that they have more children and the poor have fewer. The tax rate and the tax credit can be adjusted, considering children, to achieve what is desired in this very sensitive area.

4. Law Enforcement

The law enforcement institution includes police, prosecuting attorneys, defense attorneys, judges, politicians that oversee the police, and supporting personnel. Law enforcement officials perform one of the most important functions in civilized society. They keep people within the country from being harmed by other citizens. They enforce laws and keep civil order. Because what they do is so important and because they and their families benefit from the results of their work, setting up a law enforcement organization should work fairly well. However, there is still a strong tendency for the institution to grow too large and rob families of the wealth, power, and freedom they need to survive, while not providing the needed protection.

Institution evolution has adversely impacted the police departments. Again, as in most naïvely set-up bureaucracies, policies that make the police do a poorer job also increase their budget. It follows that you must have more police if the police are made ineffective. One destructive impact has been the evolution of cowardliness and grandstanding as law-enforcement policy.

The incident at Columbine illustrates the impact of the policy of "securing the perimeter" and waiting for the press and TV to arrive. This cowardliness and grandstanding increases the visibility of the police, and undoubtedly the free advertising increases their budgets. At Columbine, two incompetent children who had already committed suicide "held off" over 800 police for several hours while their victims bled to death. [See the December 20, 1999 issue of *Time*.] One deputy sheriff actually got into a shootout with the shooters in the parking lot before they entered the school, but he did not pursue them into the building. He appeared to be more worried about his own safety than about protecting the citizens—undoubtedly, he was trained to behave the way he did. One trained professional should have been able to handle both of these inept kids, and the incident should have been stopped before it started.

The present policies of grandstanding and cowardliness cause police departments to receive more money and to grow, so they are spreading rapidly. In the past, police officers have been paid to risk their lives for the citizens as necessary. Today they fail to do this, and Columbine clearly demonstrates the results of this failure.

The policy of being super-safe at work is much more widespread than just police departments. By super-safe, I mean the chance of getting hurt at work is at least ten times less than the chance of getting hurt traveling to and from work. The super-safe requirements come from institution-growth pressure, and not just from the industry for which the requirements were set up but from the legal profession, the government safety bureaucracies, and other naïvely set-up bureaucracies that exist in our female-dominated society because of the insatiable female need for security and safety (See Appendix).

The legal profession benefits from the money it takes from society for handling (and sometimes instigating) the litigation caused by accidents or mistakes in the line of duty. In response to the increasing possibility of being sued, super-safety is enforced in nearly every industry. The government safety bureaucracies, such as OSHA, grow by adding more safety requirements, since, as more safety requirements are put in place, a larger bureaucracy is needed to enforce the additional rules. Safety, while necessary at some level, often makes it more difficult to get the job done, and the resultant slowdown in productivity ensures that any institution will have to grow as it becomes safer at doing its job.

Part of the solution to this problem is for all people to recognize that 1) some tasks are inherently dangerous, 2) safety costs time and money, and 3) being super-safe is unnecessary and wasteful. To counteract this problem in police departments, women need to be removed from the criminal apprehension part of police work. They should also be removed from the physical aspects of fire fighting and from combat in the military. These jobs require men's willingness to act quickly in the face of personal danger not women's need to figure out the safest and securest methods. They also need to be removed from the committees that form the policies concerning these inherently dangerous, rapidly changing activities.

The largest abuse to families that grows out of the institution of law enforcement is the enforcement of unnecessary or overly restrictive laws. (Of course, other institutions that usually control and fund law enforcement make these laws and need to be addressed as well.) The laws that are most damaging to the family are ones that "protect" people from themselves, children from their parents, and spouses from each other.

Good people—sometimes a large segment of the population—often disobey unnecessary laws. Therefore, unnecessary laws make a great deal of activity (and money) for the law enforcement industry. The speed trap is a classic example. The speed limit is set lower than is necessary for safety, and good, safe drivers are tempted to disobey the law. When they do, they pay the price. Unfortunately, society as a whole pays the biggest price in the unnecessary loss of freedom and in loss of respect for lawmakers and law enforcement. The unnecessary incarceration of a family member is very damaging to a family, especially when that family member is a parent.

To many people, drug laws are like speed traps. The politicians will never repeal anti-drug laws, but not for the reasons you think. Half the criminals in jail are there because of drug violations, so half of the law enforcement institution would be eliminated if drugs where made legal. Of course the illegal drug institution (the opposite side of the coin) also wants drugs to be kept illegal, so they can continue to charge high prices and avoid paying taxes. If currently illegal drugs were legalized, they would become part of the legal-drug industry, which is regulated and taxed. No doubt, illegal drug money is supporting some anti-drug politicians to keep government bodies from legalizing those drugs.

Clearly, all illegal drugs, and especially popular illegal drugs, should be tested for both short-term and long-term effects on people. The resultant data should be available to everyone, especially doctors. With this information, there would be no more reason for drugs to be illegal for adults than for tobacco or alcohol to be illegal. If the government wants to spend money on the drug problem, then it should do so by determining the real dangers presented by illegal drugs and by truthfully informing the public. Lack of knowledge about illegal drugs has lead to the present use of scare-tactic ad campaigns that are often based on misinformation and only make people distrust public service "education" in general.

The fact that research into the effects of illegal drugs is outlawed is a clear indication of an effort to protect certain institutions like the illegal-drug-fighting law-enforcement bureaucracy, the legal drug industry, and the illegal drug industry, rather than to protect the people from themselves. This area is a classic example of politicians claiming they are trying to protect children and irresponsible adults while, in reality, they are protecting the institutions from which they derive power and money.

Of course, taking illegal drugs is really stupid because their effects are unknown, illegal drugs are often tainted, and it is a punishable crime. The proper and orderly legalization of drugs would have to occur over a fairly long time if only because the research to determine the long-term and short-term effects of illegal drugs will take time. However, it will also take time to teach the general population about these effects and to change the attitude that "if it is legal then it is healthy." People will need to be reminded that the definition of freedom is that ordinary citizens are allowed to make intelligent informed decisions and choices instead of the government making decisions for them.

If our population were well informed about the real dangers of drugs and if the drugs were produced by a well-regulated legal industry, the damage to our society from drug use would almost certainly be less than it is today. By legalizing drugs, we could eliminate a large portion of the law-enforcement bureaucracy, eliminate a large amount of organized crime, and greatly reduce the need for incarceration institutions. A large segment of the population has a low regard for our society because drugs are illegal, so making drugs legal would increase their respect for authority. The tax on drugs could be used to fight their use and abuse through truthful advertising and research. Remember: necessity (often for security and safety) is always the argument used by tyrants to destroy freedom. Thus, on any issues like this, we should err on the side of freedom.

Our method of selling certain legal drugs "by prescription only" has been set up mostly to enhance the pharmaceutical industry and the medical institutions, both of which make considerably more money from prescription control than from over-the-counter (OTC) remedies. It is true that most people, at least initially, need a doctor's help to determine whether to use a particular drug to treat a particular ailment. However, adults should be allowed to judge when they or their children need the doctor's help.

In Mexico, most drugs can be bought across the counter without a prescription, yet there is no evidence that this has caused excessive drug abuse or a negative impact on healthcare. Unless we feel that the Mexican population has vastly superior judgment in these matters than the US population, there is no real reason to have prescription requirements. American anti-drug laws are passed based on arguments that appeal to elitism. The population has been convinced that a large number of irresponsible people will abuse drugs if they are made legal or their control by prescription is stopped. We must reason our way out of this elitist trap.

Another abuse by the government is the power of the police department to immediately confiscate property on suspicion of crime, as in drug laws, or to keep fines from arrests they make. Allowing the confiscation of property when a crime has not been proven in court causes a rapid evolution toward tyranny. This practice would be ruled in violation of the due process clause of the Constitution if the judges were not also part of the corrupt institution. As with the local bureaucracies supporting small-town speed traps, the entire American law enforcement bureaucracy is involved in this miscarriage of justice.

The evolution of law enforcement has led to extremely lenient sentencing of repeat criminals. The more criminals there are and the more crimes they commit, the larger the law enforcement bureaucracy must become. Some people now recognize this problem and, by referendum, are enacting "three strikes and you are out" laws that have greatly reduced crime. Criminals who are kept in jail do not commit more crimes or lead others into a life of crime. The threat of this stronger punishment also deters crime. The politicians generally avoid enacting tough sentencing rules because high crime justifies increased taxes for larger bureaucracies, and not nearly all of the increase goes to law enforcement. More criminals also mean more defense lawyers who contribute to the election campaigns of all the judges, prosecuting attorneys, and politicians. Thus, more crime means more money, power, and prestige for every institution involved. The only real loser is society as a whole—in more ways than just handing over our hard-earned cash to support the institutions and their beneficiaries.

Police departments have both male and female officers. Reacting properly to stop violent crime and making arrests are natural impulses for a male cop. Reacting properly to domestic conflicts is a natural impulse for a female cop. As with other jobs, and especially dangerous jobs like police and fire protection, the mixing of men and women in the workplace should be avoided (as discussed in Chapter 1 on higher education and in Chapter 6 on business).

Helping each other in dangerous situations is a particularly bonding experience, and for the sake of spouses and children of married police officers, male and female cops should avoid working together. The natural division of labor should be adhered to, since men normally do the more dangerous hunting-protecting tasks (such as catching violent criminals) while women are better at nurturing and reconciling tasks (such as victim care and domestic confrontation amelioration—which is still very dangerous).

Recently, law-making and law-enforcement institutions have been usurping the power of individuals, especially males, and legislating morality by redefining crimes that have strong emotional appeal (such as rape, domestic violence, child abuse, etc.) to include a broader range of behaviors. This redefinition of crimes increases the statistics of occurrence of the crime, which justifies, to the uninformed masses, the existence of (and need of more money for) institutions such as DHHS and abused women's care, in addition to law enforcement.

A prime example is rape. Rape is a much worse crime than assault or battery because it robs the victim of sexual purity, reproduction rights, and the power of sex appeal. Except for this robbery, rape should be treated as battery with no special laws. It is true that rape spoils the victim's ability to interact with the opposite sex, but almost all violent crimes affect our ability to interact socially, so I consider the actual significant social-interaction effect of rape to be the robbery of sexual purity, especially destruction of one's self-image. Boys forcing a broom handle into the rectum of another boy are not committing rape since there is no robbery. It is perverted battery, and it should be punished, but it is not rape, and it should not be referred to as such.

With the rise of BEEism, rape is being considered a greater and greater crime compared to battery, while adultery is being considered less and less immoral. Adultery is not even a crime in most areas of the U.S., yet adultery robs the spouse (victim) of sexual purity and reproduction rights much as rape robs its victim. This increased acceptance of adultery is another family-extinguishing value. It was punishable by death in ancient times, which may be a bit severe, but it certainly should not be accepted as moral behavior today.

The difference is that BEEs want females to be able to use the animalistic power derived from their sex appeal. They want women to become whores in their quest for power and money. This is why BEEs see nothing wrong with female interns having sex with powerful male politicians. This is why adultery is being ignored, while rape is being considered more and more egregious. Other people also support the increased punishment for rape because they desire more punishment for crime in general, want to protect women, and understand the loss of sexual purity and reproduction rights (which both men and women also suffer through adultery, though no one wants to recognize or deal justly with this).

Even greater than the robbery of purity in rape is the production of a child through adultery. Not only is it breaking the marriage vows and robbing the spouse, as described above, but also it is reproducing the genes of an irresponsible cheater instead of reproducing the genes of a responsible, loyal person.

In the past, sexual purity and reproduction rights were important, and using the power of sex appeal was considered immoral. Then it was not possible for a person to be raped by a faithful spouse or faithful consensual sex partner. Rape did not apply to prostitutes and extremely promiscuous people. Any forced sex was still battery, illegal, and punishable by law, but these cases were not classified as rape. The slide of our society backward, to the use of female sex appeal as a means of persuasion, is degrading to women and abusive to men.

Sexual purity is extremely valuable, not only for control of venereal diseases, but also for true, life-long bonding to a spouse or future spouse. However, to BEEs any personal characteristic other than education level and power over others is not recognized as valuable. Since they do not recognize sexual purity or the male sex drive, they will often say that rape is, above all, a power issue. They, with the help of lawmakers and law enforcers, try to attach rape to any sexual interaction that a woman says she did not like. This allows women to use their sex appeal for the maximum power and self-benefit. Unfortunately, many of these BEEs are in positions of authority and their ideas are accepted.

We must stop listening to these BEEs whose ideas serve the institutions of higher education, law enforcement, and big business rather than the welfare of our families. Married couples must develop a common moral code (probably with the help of religion) and become the servants of a higher Good who is both the alpha-male and the alpha-female. This will give both male and female humans maximum happiness. They should write their own marriage contracts that maximize the benefits of marriage to themselves and their children. This can partially neutralize the state laws concerning marriage and domestic relations that serve other evolved institutions and destroy the family.

For example, if a woman agrees to the man being the head of the house, then he will become a lieutenant. (See Appendix for definition) The family then becomes his responsibility and he can easily work hard for the family because in this situation it is the natural response. When the man is a lieutenant, his natural goal is to take care of his woman and children and to keep them happy, healthy, and secure. On the other hand, if a woman insists on being in charge, her man is relegated to the oppressed sub-class. For the man to take responsibility now becomes very difficult. His natural response is to revolt and kill the oppressor or to leave. He will not take care of the family and may revolt in any number of family-extinguishing behaviors. Thus, both men and women will get more of what they want and need if men give women input in family decisions but women give their men the final word, as in a traditional marriage.

Unfortunately, in our BEE-dominated society, it is very difficult for a woman to treat her man correctly because of her conflicting need to follow the tenets of society. We must recognize that the needs of men are different from those of women. In general, the traditional rules are better for men, women, and families. There is no greater joy for a man than to provide the security needs of the woman he loves. There is no greater joy for a woman than to have her security needs provided by the man she loves. We must not allow BEEs or the government to rob us of this joy. The new BEE "morality" serves only our pathologically evolved institutions, not our families.

The crime of domestic violence is also being used to destroy marriage and the family. Increasingly more domestic confrontations are being defined as criminal. Couples and families should be allowed the maximum amount of freedom in resolving disputes. Each marriage partner needs to define an allowable level of expression of anger he or she can tolerate from his or her spouse. Too low of an allowable level is unhealthy ... too high can be dangerous. Clearly, this should be agreed upon before marriage. The legal level where the police can step in uninvited should be high. Thus, domestic violence should not be criminal unless serious harm (for example, requiring medical attention or leaving a permanent mark) is purposely inflicted. Remember, we are discussing uninvited police intervention. At any time, adults who feel they are in danger should be able to call the police to be removed from the situation, even if nobody has touched them.

Some police departments have a domestic violence policy that is brutal and absurd. Namely, for all domestic violence calls, somebody must be arrested. Calls relating to domestic violence should be no different than other calls. Sometimes there is an arrest, and sometimes there is not. Repeated callers for false alarms in any situation need special treatment, case by case.

I consider it immoral for a spouse to inflict physical harm on his or her mate, but it should not be criminal unless it is serious, as defined above. Corporal punishment is the most natural and perhaps best discipline for children, as discussed in Chapter 2. Excessive or wrongly administered corporal punishment is immoral but should not be considered criminal unless it meets the criteria given above.

Presently, slamming a door is considered domestic violence and may be criminal. This is stupid. While acting aggressively is becoming criminal, the non-violent, just as immoral, behaviors of adultery, divorce, and verbal abuse are being tolerated as completely acceptable. This shows how powerful BEEism has become. Those who are more highly educated are more adept at verbal abuse and provoking physical violence, which, punishable by an arrest record, is the most effective passive-aggressive way to get back at someone they don't like. Unfortunately, passive-aggressive behavior, though it causes many violent crimes, isn't even a misdemeanor.

A sure sign of tyranny is governmental usurpation of the rights of parents to raise their children. The Nazis took over the rearing of the children, and the Communists begin "educating" their children when they are very young. In the name of helping the children, but in reality to grow the bureaucracy and to implant pro-bureaucracy ideals, the government is usurping the parents' power and right to raise their children properly.

Influenced by BEEism, our own government has outlawed discipline, morals, respect for parents, and parental control of the family. Teenagers very often threaten to call the police if their parents don't stop attempting to discipline them, and it works. This destruction of parental authority, or even the possibility that it might be diminished, is very damaging to the family. Children should never be taken from the parents unless the parent has to go to jail.

Preventing good people from rearing their children properly is extremely damaging to society. Not only is a whole generation being spoiled, but also many potentially excellent parents are not having children because they know they will not have the authority to rear them properly.

The excuse for this destructive insertion of the government into the family is to protect children that are in danger of serious harm from their parents. In reality, it is just the evolution of bureaucracy (in law enforcement and in human services) and the enforcement of the immoral philosophies of other evolved institutions. The damage to society inflicted by undermining the authority of good parents is much greater than the good that might be derived from "saving" already damaged children. When these children are taken out of supposedly abusive homes, they are put into a foster care system that is, in many cases, a more abusive environment than the home from which the children were taken.

Public recognition of what is going on is the first step to a solution to this problem. Everyone must remember that institution evolution does not care about anyone or anything but institution growth, even when the institution is composed entirely of kind, compassionate, and moral people. Their opinions of what is good and moral are products of institution evolution. Once we all fully understand and believe this, we can stop the tyranny of institution evolution and prevent the extinction of our families.

Our ancestors have survived thousands of generations of rearing children as taught by their own parents. There is chemistry between natural parents and children that almost always prevents abuse. Therefore, people should be left alone in rearing their natural children, and control of this process by a government bureaucracy, perverted by institution evolution, should not be allowed.

The usurpation of parental authority by the government has been a factor in the enactment of patronizing laws. Since the parents have lost control of their children, they cannot stop them from destructive behavior. They then support laws so the government will enforce proper behavior. These laws restrict the freedom of everyone. Examples of patronizing laws that are strongly supported by weakened parents are curfews, helmet laws, seatbelt laws, and drug laws.

The illusion that there is a great deal of abuse by natural parents stems from a combination of institution propaganda (for instance from child protection agencies) and our own elitist tendency to believe other parents are inferior to us. The fact is that adults who are not the natural parents of the children are much more likely to inflict serious child abuse. For example, "in Britain, a child whose biological mother cohabits was 73 time more likely to suffer fatal abuse than a child with married parents." [Robert Whalen, *Broken Homes & Battered Children,* 1993] In American bureaucracies, however, the distinction between natural parents and other adults is blurred in reporting child abuse for propaganda against parents, especially fathers.

If we are serious about child abuse, we should be working much harder to stop the breakup of families. This means we must recognize and reverse the tyranny of the legal profession, psychiatry, higher education, business, and government, which rob children of their natural parents through the insidious destruction of marriage and resultant divorces. For instance, instead of financial downsides to marriage (higher taxes, higher benefit costs, etc.), there should be divorce penalties. Also, it should be illegal for either divorced parent to bring a new sexual companion into the home environment of the children. There is a powerful animalistic instinct for the new most powerful male to mate with all unrelated females and to oppress the smaller males. Therefore, an unrelated new male companion is a strong candidate for behaviors such as molestation and abuse of the divorcee's children. Likewise, a new unrelated female companion may be tempted to consort with younger males and to assert her power over the young females that she feels may be competing with her for alpha status. We cannot continue to ignore this instinct.

Closely related to the overblown "child abuse" problem is spousal abuse. Some people define abuse as "any consistent behavior used to control another person". Under this definition, normal, good parenting with well-defined limits for children and well-defined punishment when children exceed those limits would be considered abuse. Under this definition, people living in a normal relationship and consistently communicating what they need from the relationship are abusive. This is not abuse; it is normal life. Again, the BEEs try to outlaw and render immoral the animalistic behavior-control mechanisms, such as anger and physical force, while strengthening the animalistic mental- and emotional-manipulation mechanisms such as withdrawal, sex appeal, and provocative verbal disrespect.

5. The Evolution and Impact of Entertainment and the Media

While higher education and the government are the sources of many family extinguishing-values, the media is the main teacher of these values to the general population. The media is particularly bent on bashing fathers, degrading motherhood and women, and promoting promiscuity, adultery, divorce, and the gay lifestyle. All are very anti-family values.

In order to sell entertainment, producers must make it different from ho-hum everyday experiences. This is why violence, sex, and superheroes are so dominant. Unfortunately, the more time one spends involved with the fiction of entertainment, the more it changes one's perception of what is normal or everyday. Thus, for the entertainment to be emotionally pleasurable, the sex and violence must become more graphic and immoral and the superheroes more and more super. This, of course, continues to corrupt one's feelings about what is normal or moral—what is acceptable, just, and fair behavior—let alone what is uplifting as opposed to what is degrading.

Those who spend the largest portion of time being entertained are the ones in the most danger. Even though the entertainment is fiction, it changes intuitions, feelings, and perceptions about almost everything. The worst part is that the entertainment industry is not being held accountable for portraying lies, even though the perceptions they influence govern many people's lives, especially those of women.

A good example of the influence of entertainment is the public's perception of violent crime. While actual violent crime has been dramatically decreasing from 1991 to 2005, violence in the media was increasing, and opinion polls show that most people thought that violent crime was increasing. The amount of violence people see or hear about in their real lives is much smaller than what they see in entertainment, so the public opinion about violence is based almost entirely upon fiction. Some influence, of course, is due to the news media, which, to make up for a lack of real local viewer-drawing news, bombard us via repetitive news broadcasts and newspaper and magazine headlines with nearly every act of violence in the entire world. Thus, American public opinion of violent crime is based on fictional and worldwide perceptions rather than local reality. What is really stupid, though, is that people seem willing to give up their freedoms to combat this false perception of violence.

Here's an example of how brainless our intuition has become about movies. The other day, in a movie that I watched on an airplane, an approximately 7-year-old boy pointed a loaded gun at his parents to make them squirm. Pointing a loaded gun at another human, let alone at your own parents, is about the most immoral behavior possible for a human being. However, Hollywood thinks it is fine, though in the same movie, they would not dare allow someone to say "shit." Obviously the moral values of Hollywood, which have been declining for some time, are now completely out of control.

Beyond its obvious amorality, however, the greatest threat to our society from entertainment is the propaganda it contains that has changed the way we feel about everything from lying to homosexuality. The present rating systems are a joke because they only rate the overt affronts to some people's sensibilities—the same things that draw others to the box office (sex, violence, and "adult" themes). They completely ignore the propaganda that is destroying our values, culture, and families. We should have a more complete rating system for entertainment to show how it will influence us.

From my point of view, most entertainment today denies the difference between men and women, and it demonizes black, Asian, and Germanic men. It denigrates adults, marriage, parenthood, and parents, especially fathers. It demonizes Christian religions and especially Catholicism. It promotes women, feminism, divorce, homosexuals, promiscuity, dishonesty, Godlessness, mysticism, and spiritism. For example, Christian church music played in the background while a psychotic killer is on the screen associates the Christian religion with psychotic killers. The race (color) or creed of a hero promotes that race or creed, while the race or creed of "the bad guy" puts down that race or creed. Stories of dealings with the spirits of the dead undermine the Bible's teachings about death. Rather than uplifting those things that are most helpful to the health of families, the propaganda agenda of Hollywood promotes the lifestyles, the morals, and the beliefs of the people that own and run Hollywood, including the critics. These people are mostly BEEs, and Hollywood is a consistent and powerful instiller of anti-family values.

Some organization, perhaps religious organizations, should publish ratings of the propaganda contents of the products of the entertainment industry. A rating of the probable effects of the propaganda in a particular movie, TV show, video game, or music album concerning the viewer's feeling toward different people, religions, behaviors, lifestyles, etc., could be given. Since all entertainment contains some type of propaganda, parents could check the scores to choose for their children entertainment that promotes what they consider correct. They can also stay away from entertainment that contains propaganda that might damage their children by instilling family-extinguishing values. Finally, the propaganda rating system might awaken society to the overall impact that entertainment has on society as a whole. For example, the movie *Kindergarten Cop* contains strong propaganda against fathers. Such a rating system would alert fathers to keep their children away from the movie. As a father, I consider this a very immoral movie because of its anti-father propaganda. Not to pick on Arnold Schwarzenegger, but *Jingle All the Way* is another, though slightly more disguised, father-bashing movie. The worst effect of movies like these is the instillation of negative feelings towards fatherhood, which is anti-family.

Rating the propaganda impact of entertainment would help people to realize what is happening. For now, however, pre-viewing media to which your children may be exposed is essential, and limiting exposure to fictional entertainment is the best defense against the false perceptions developed by fiction. One video game OR movie OR TV show per week should be the maximum—certainly no more than one "electronic entertainment" period per day. Parents should make it a habit to recognize and intellectualize what a movie, music video, television program, or video game is doing to its viewers. They must teach their children about the immoral behavior and propaganda in entertainment, and they can start with TV commercials and the actions of characters in TV shows.

Advertising is a big source of unhappiness that is destroying families. In order for big business to sell products, advertising must create a need for the product, convince you that you are unhappy, instill within you the expectation that you should always be filled with happiness, and show you that their product will fill you with happiness. The biggest negative impact is that advertising turns us in to good consumers in general. Namely, they convince us that we are unhappier than we think we should be and we think buying something will make it better. Unfortunately, thinking we're unhappier makes us unhappier indeed, and the feedback effect on some people is devastating, including blaming this unhappiness on other family members, which often leads to divorce of parents or revolt of children, all of which weakens and can destroy a family.

Advertisements, TV shows, and movies often undermine parental authority by displaying children behaving as adults and parents, especially fathers, behaving as children. This is done because it is easy to convince a child to want a product, so the next logical step is to put the child in charge of making the decision to buy the product. This role-reversing propaganda is very damaging to the family because parents need respect from their children to raise them properly, but this propaganda makes it more difficult for children to listen to their parents and more difficult for parents to enforce correct behavior. When parents see such propaganda, they need to voice their disapproval to its source and prevent their children from being exposed to it.

When we understand the point of entertainment institutional evolution, we can minimize its influence on us, though it is too powerful to neutralize entirely. The political propaganda put on TV has been discussed and well publicized; yet, it continues and is very effective. The powerful impact of simultaneous audio and visual sensory input to the brain does not leave enough mental capacity to rationally filter the propaganda in real time. Just sit down beside the TV sometime when people are watching and look at their faces. They look like zombies. Their brains are fully occupied with taking in the sensations. There is little or no capacity left for critical or creative thinking.

No one can completely neutralize the emotional impact on our intuition of continuous sensory bombardment upon our perceptions. I have never had a good idea while watching TV. TV is the most massive waste of brainpower in the world. For this reason alone, political material on TV and in movies should be very restricted, especially within a few months of an election.

In addition to being too powerful, most of the TV political "information" does very little to really inform the voter concerning important issues. The Constitution of the United States of America guarantees freedom of the press and free speech but not the freedom of sensory bombardment by the electromagnetic radiation of the airwaves. The written word can be pondered as we read it, unlike the powerful irrational emotional attack on our perceptions that is the result of electronic auditory and visual stimulation. Radio is not as mind-consuming (since the visual stimulus is absent) and could be allowed. Audio discourse with a blank screen or a picture without sound or animation might be allowed on TV. A ten-second silent pause for reflection should be required at the beginning and end of each political presentation. Otherwise, interweaving or close proximity in time of full bombardment could defeat the blank screen or still picture. It takes a while for the brain to start thinking again after it has been rendered useless by the sensory bombardment of TV or movies.

Kennedy's defeat of Nixon in 1960 through their debates on television showed that whomever controls the media controls the elections. Very soon after this event, the process of selecting the candidates from each party was changed. Before this happened, each state chose representatives for the parties' national conventions. These representatives at the national conventions chose the candidates. Now most representatives are forced by law to vote for the candidate that wins the popular vote of the statewide primary. Therefore, the media also controls the candidates' selection, since most people get to "know" the candidates through the media. Thus, consistent with institution evolution, the media is now controlling politics to give itself more power.

By carefully choosing what they show and what they don't show, the media can project nearly any image they want of a particular candidate. When something comes to light that might defeat the media's agenda, their "political analysts" comment on the incident, portraying it in the best possible light (called putting their own spin on it). Because of media manipulation of the candidates' exposure, the candidates' own acting while in front of the cameras, and the "spin" of media analysts, people learn very little about the candidates through TV. Thus, the media pretty much controls the primaries and the elections. They make sure no candidate wins the primary that might support the working family, like Howard Dean. It was amazing to see how TV destroyed Howard Dean with just body language and innuendo. The media owners and controllers have become the ruling oligarchy of this country, with their main control apparent in the primaries. Once they have their two candidates, the goal is a close election to maximize the profit generated from the election coverage. Not only does the media control who wins; they also control by how much.

People were better served by the old system of electing local people they know personally to represent them in finding out about the candidates and making the right choice. Better to have people who are known and trusted by those who elected them selecting a candidate they actually know, than our present media-controlled mockery of democracy.

The American people have lost control of the government, and politics is now a battle between the people who are struggling to control the media, which in turn controls the government. The actual owners of the media are businessmen, and media must please business to garner advertising from business. On the other hand, the media professionals are mostly BEEs. Thus, big business and BEEs, the two groups that are perhaps the most destructive to our families and the next generation, control the media and politics. The Republican Party is essentially run by the business power in the media, and the Democratic Party is run by the BEE power in the media. They both lie to the people to win elections, and neither really represents very many people, but both have the potential for horrific tyranny.

We must break the stranglehold the media has on politics and hence our government. The first thing to do after returning to candidate selection by party convention is to outlaw the overly powerful audiovisual media from politics as discussed above. Outlawing the full power of TV from politics is an extreme measure, but we have an extreme problem. I am sure the Congress and the President are frustrated by the control of the non-elected ruling oligarchy, and with one quick act, Congress could regain control of the government.

Another measure is to break up the media. Presently, the media is owned by a handful of large conglomerates controlled by a few people. For democracy to function properly, voters must know the truth. The first amendment to the Constitution, freedom of press and freedom of speech, is designed to restrain the government from controlling the information obtained by voters, because by selectively misinforming the voters, the government could soon destroy all freedom and the system would fail. Clearly, these like-thinking people that own all the media have defeated the intent of the first amendment and we are now ruled by an immoral oligarchy, the net effect of which is the impoverishment and extinguishing of our families.

Free press, with a large number of independent sources, is the best way to develop the flow of truthful information to the people, because unreliable or incomplete sources are soon exposed for what they are and consequently ignored. The amount of media that can be owned by a corporation, an individual, or any associated group should, therefore, be very limited by law. Maybe the internet can provide this diversity, but it is difficult to know your source when you surf the net and it requires considerable effort to be sure you are gathering reliable information. Obama's success in using this medium to help his campaign clearly demonstrates that the internet has a large role to play in politics. We do need to be vigilant, or the ruling oligarchy will gain control of the internet through some contrived excuse like controlling pornography. The oligarchy is also working on controlling search engines. Control of information sources must be as loose as possible.

Unfortunately, of course, the media-controlled government in the U.S.A. is now moving away from a large number of independent sources. Laws that once limited ownership of the media were nullified by the Telecommunications Act of 1996, demonstrating that the media conglomerates control the government. [See Bill Moyer's *Free Speech for Sale* on PBS.] Finding the truth in what is being reported is becoming more and more difficult, and trustworthy information sources are almost non-existent. Presently, the owners of the media have regular meetings with each other. Many wild conspiracy theories are floating around because most of the media is only interested in pushing the agenda of those in control and not interested in telling the truth. When there is no source for the truth the only thing left is wild speculation, which is very dangerous.

The truth that is essential for the survival of our republic is no longer available. We need laws that limit media ownership and prevent the separate owners from working together. This would diffuse the control so that the truth might be published, and all sides of every issue presented fairly.

Finally, we must hope and pray that the educated soon recognize the source of BEEism and its immoral dogma. At least they should recognize it as a religion with no place in politics. Unfortunately, its enforcement appears to be the first goal of the Democratic Party, even though the party could strengthen its position with the general public by removing the BEE litmus test in all states and by making true advocacy for the working people and restraint of big business its first priority. The Democrats presently take the immoral side of most moral issues (which should not even be in politics) and the Republicans are effectively using this against them. The working people have two bad choices: go with the BEE Democrats and extinguish your family in a couple of generations, or go with the Republicans and live in abject poverty in a couple of generations. Many are correctly choosing poverty over extinction. The successful 2006 campaign indicated that the Democrats might be changing in the correct direction. In 2008 they were quiet about their anti-family values, because they know many people are pro-family, and won the election. However, it remains to be seen if they will try to enforce by law the anti-family BEE values that many of them still hold.

One way of making the political parties more responsive to the people is to increase the chances of success for third parties. Instead of just voting for one candidate, voters should be allowed to rank the candidates for each office. The vote-counting computers could then eliminate losing candidates and automatically change votes for those candidates' to the voter's next preference until there are just two candidates and the winner would be the one with a majority. People could then vote for their favorite candidate without "wasting" their vote because if their first choice was a clear loser, their second choice would count. This would also prevent third-party candidates from spoiling elections—taking votes from candidates who without a third-party candidate in the running might have won by a clear majority. Examples of such spoilers are Ralph Nader in 2000, Ross

Perot in 1992, and Teddy Roosevelt in 1912. I mention the 1912 election because it was after this spoiled election that the devastating 16th and 17th amendments were passed by a minority government.

Any change in voting, however, will have to be done by some referendum process, because both parties benefit from the present system and are unlikely to make any movement toward changing it.

6. The Impact of Big Business

One of the beauties of free enterprise business is that making a profit and increasing business are honest goals. Other institutions that unwittingly evolve into automatons whose only purpose is to amass money and power (for instance, government and education) are much more dangerous because the perverted values produced by the evolution of these institutions are cloaked as some new morality. Business, on the other hand, exists only to make money, and everyone knows it.

Now, the elitists of higher education and government look down on business as money–grubbing, when, in fact, essentially all institutions are also power-mongers and money-grubbers. The only difference is that only in business do people recognize the real source of their policies. In business, the changes required for making more money are more honest and open and can be more quickly instituted because they are intelligence-guided. However, some subtle effects of business evolution need to be pointed out.

Since the world has become full of democracies, governments have started regulating big business to prevent the abuse of people and the environment. This lowers the power and wealth of business. To defeat this control, the present tactic of business is to engage in trade treaties. Much money and propaganda are being used to establish free trade with no tariffs or regulations to control business. Through their control of the media, business has been able to sell the idea that tariffs are worse than taxes. The truth is that taxes are bad for the economy and tariffs are just targeted taxes that are also bad for the economy. The argument that tariffs have a special way of hurting the economy is baseless. Removing tariffs won't help the economy any more by than removing any other tax.

The real reason big business wants free trade is to defeat government regulation and to defeat unions. The treaties themselves disallow some regulations, and the completely free flow of trade allows the companies to engage, in a country where they are allowed, in immoral activities disallowed in the U.S.A. Free trade lets immorally manufactured products move freely and be sold worldwide. As long as materials and products can move freely, businesses can just move to another country if the unions strike where they are currently located. Free trade weakens the sovereignty of nations and transfers massive amounts of power from the governments and the people (if it is a democracy) to corporations and to the world government organizations that enforce the treaties. If this trend continues, the powerful corporations, with their control of the media, will evolve into the tyrants that they were at the turn of the previous century, with most of our families living in abject poverty and with both parents working 60 hours a week just to survive.

If business makes too much profit, it destroys the consumer base and the economy, just as surely as over-taxation by the government. Most of the fruits of their labors must be returned to workers so enough money will be in the hands of consumers for the economy to grow. The fact that many big companies like Microsoft and IBM have tens of billions of dollars in excess cash indicates that they're taking too much profit. They can find no advantageous place to invest their excess cash because not enough of companies' profits are going to workers to create demand for products produced by companies that could then give profitable returns to investors. Over-taxation by the government and/or too much profit by industry are big causes of economic recession. For a healthy economy, we must have strong labor unions to limit excess profits and a pro-family political party to control the government to limit excessive taxation. This will also support a strong middle class and decrease poverty. The Democratic Party used to stand for both of these principles, but now its primary focus is on enforcing pro-choice abortion, removing children and authority from families, maintaining taxation levels, outlawing guns, and supporting the gay lifestyle—all family-extinguishing values.

A business-controlled world government is growing in power and enforcing global tyranny. Any country that tries to prevent Western big business and supporting BEE moral values from invading is annihilated by NATO or UN bombs—figuratively and literally. The democracies of the world are becoming powerless symbolic organizations. BEEs support this globalization because they want a world government that will enforce their family-extinguishing values worldwide. Most of the business- and BEE-controlled media are supporting this takeover.

These takeovers are often "justified" as necessary to prevent human rights violations. The main violations of concern are women's rights and freedom of media ownership. Western business people and BEEs will totally exploit a country when they own the media that can control the women, who are empowered by the so-called women's rights movements to control the country. Institution evolution demands that women have the political power because they are easily controlled with their need for security and with their need to please the powerful. (See the Appendix.) If freeing the country, instead of oppressive exploitation, were the goal then there would be concerns about the right to bear arms. The outlawing of private gun ownership, which is almost always instituted along with a NATO or UN takeover, is a clear sign that the result will be oppression and exploitation by Western elitists, not true freedom and lieutenant status for all. If human rights violations were really a concern, we would not be trading with China.

The rapid destruction of all other cultures and religions by BEEism and big business produces an environment ripe for the growth of terrorist organizations like al Qaida. The despicable September 11, 2001, attack was a misguided desperate attempt of brave men to save their culture and religion. They struck at the heart of the strongest leaders of their attackers. The global domination by Western big business was symbolized by the World Trade Center, and the Pentagon symbolizes U.S. military power, which enforces this domination. They just didn't realize that the attack was the wrong approach and is only going to speed their demise. The point, however, is that opening of borders around the globe by big business to prevent government control of their marauding exploitation of the world also makes it very difficult for governments to control equally marauding, criminal organizations like al Qaida.

While radical Islamic fundamentalism is not the most wonderful religion/culture, at least it does not murder children, destroy families, and commit genocide of intelligence, as our BEE religion/culture does. From a Darwinian perspective, Islamic fundamental values are superior because people with these values have survived hundreds of years while people with BEE values self-extinguish in a few generations. Islam is growing in part as a response to the attacks of our institutions on the family and especially on fathers. Fortunately, we still have the constitution, which should protect us in our attempt to change our misdirection without bloodshed.

Since institution evolution is a correct (provable, repeatable) model, the democracies of the world must move quickly to kill the growth of world government or it will evolve into the most oppressive of all tyrants. It will make the Hitler and Stalin regimes look like picnics, since there seems to be no real power against it. Once it evolves to some critical level of power, it will be unstoppable, and eventually it will impose total tyranny on the world. With the help of modern computers and communication systems, a handful of self-proclaimed demigods will rule the world and live in luxury, while everyone else will be enslaved and live in extreme poverty and squalor. Before you say that it will never happen, think back over what has been the historical state of the vast majority of human existence: tyranny and poverty, with relatively few shining moments of democracy and widespread prosperity.

The critical level of power is unknown, and it may already be too late. It has already overpowered both major political parties in this country and is growing exponentially. This is the new world order. The reason business can take power from politicians is that business owns the media. The politicians need to limit the power of the media by breaking it up and removing the full power of television from politics as discussed in Chapter 5.

We must all be more diligent and more aware of institution evolution. We must become more critical and less gullible! This is not a conspiracy; it is just uncontrolled natural institution evolution. It is not due to evil people conspiring to take over. Rather, it is due to good but complacent and/or ignorant people doing nothing—the "don't worry, be happy" syndrome.

Big business wants women in the workplace because they are more easily controlled than men and because working women and men can be turned against each other. The story goes that Henry Ford hired a large number of black workers hoping to destroy the unions. He did not think blacks and whites could make a strong union together. He was wrong and the attempt failed. Now, however, The Rockefeller Foundation is a big supporter of "women's rights". And why does big business support co-mingling of men and women in the work place? Because this co-mingling does break unions. What's the evidence of this? As women's power has grown, the unions have weakened, the poor are getting poorer, and the rich are getting richer.

Remember that women need security and have more of a need to please powerful males and females than do men. (See the Appendix.) Their peacekeeping, non-confrontational nature interferes with the male characteristic of hate of elitist suppressors and the male tendency to revolt against oppression that made unions possible. Their inability to form strong unions is the main reason women are paid less than men. If the women's rights movement were truly designed for normal women, then it would work harder to get higher pay for jobs that require the natural nurturing skills that women possess, such as nurses, patient care technicians, teachers, housekeepers, cooks, servers, and day-care workers.

Increasing the number of women in the workplace also increases the size of the work force. Thus, for big business, co-mingling the work force seems to be a dream come true. The work force becomes larger and unorganized, so wages and salaries will be lower.

In the long term, however, big business will suffer from women in the workplace. More workers and lower wages may help next quarter's profits, but a co-mingled work force is less productive because of the increased strain on marriages and the lack of work-related communication abilities between men and women. When both parents work, the total productivity outside the family does not increase much because so much energy and time are required to rear a family. If the wife has a job, then the husband must work more at home, which makes him more tired and, therefore, less productive at work. The total production of these two adults for big business is far less than twice the productivity of a worker with a relaxing home life. The children, about whom no one but the parents really care, are robbed of whatever extra productivity is extracted from their home. And don't forget that working women have fewer children, so the number of workers needed for our future labor market will be deficient.

Taking care of a family is a full-time job, and the future work force will suffer from the inadequate rearing of children that is common today because both parents are working. The lack of proper rearing for children is a major disaster for this country that will become apparent after the next generation has been raised, at which point it will be too late to change. When the diminished numbers of children—and those predominately spoiled—reach the work force, big business will suffer more than it is benefiting from the present immoral abuse of women and families.

The extinction of families is squandered human capital, with the primary beneficiaries being business, government, and universities, though a slightly more opulent lifestyle is attained by the irresponsible members who are not reproducing. Societies do very well for one generation when the generation does not have replacement children because all of their work goes into "improving their life style". When this generation tries to retire, there is insufficient labor force to care for them, and they will have a miserable retirement and overburden the few children in the next generation caring for them. We need to realize now that the baby boomers may have to be euthanized when they become non-productive because they did not leave a next-generation labor force large enough to take care of them. The X-generation, which was decimated by family-extinguishing values, may take revenge and annihilate the baby boomers or at least dramatically decrease their standard of living. The irresponsible squandering of human capital that began in the 1980's in exchange for an overly opulent lifestyle will most certainly have very grave consequences for our children and could result in an early grave for many of the greedy baby boomers. The boomers that should suffer the most are the ones that did not have replacement children.

Putting women in the work force is a major assault on the family that has far more drawbacks than benefits for the family. From 1970 to 1990, the number of two-wage-earner families increased dramatically, but the standard of living actually declined. Since families are still competing for the same space and property, raising everyone's income does not improve the overall situation in these areas. However, this does impoverish the women who stay home and properly care for their families. The co-mingling of men and women in the workplace has broken the unions, so the rich are getting richer and the poor are getting poorer and the nation's median income, adjusted for inflation, is decreasing. Finally, the present tax system, which is unfair to working married couples, further diminishes their benefit from any perceived extra income. (In Chapter 3, a new tax system is proposed that would solve this problem.)

One solution to co-mingling is to emulate the concept of the home as it existed before women were thrust into the workplace. It was not that inefficient, since taking care of a family's emotional and physical needs, which included involvement in the educational and other activities of children outside the home, is more or less a fulltime job for one person. Its benefits included more parental control, less turmoil caused by children, and a more focused wage earner who was able to devote most of his (since most wage earners were male) time outside the home to earning the money needed to support this socially productive home.

One of the negative results of that old structure of the American home was that the male was often not as involved with his children as he should have been. Men are especially needed in the rearing of boys as they approach puberty and beyond. In the natural tribal environment, young males joined their fathers in the pursuit of resources and safety for the tribe. Today most boys do not have the opportunity to work with their fathers, which is the natural and best way for them to learn how to be responsible and productive adults. Working together is a more powerful bonding and teaching experience than playing together, which is all that most modern parents and children experience.

A disadvantage to the stay-at-home mom is the lack of time women spend in the company of other women. In the natural tribal environment, the women (of all ages) worked together, doing the tasks that were designated as women's work, with the young children nearby and under their watchful eyes. Modern women can get this companionship by joining parent-teach organizations, women's clubs, or other organizations; however, unless something valuable comes from these times together, these activities are not very fulfilling. Getting together for a break and gossiping about those who aren't there, won't work.

A better solution is to organize work patterns as closely as possible to the tribal situation. The men and the women both leave the house to work, but the women take the young children and the girls to work with them and the men take the school-aged boys to work with them.

Companies would hire either all men or all women. (Large companies could have male divisions of the company and female divisions, with only the top level of management co-mingled.) The ones that hire all women would provide childcare for young children and a school for girls. The ones that hire men would have a school for boys. The state government would scrutinize and subsidize these schools, with the parents of the children electing a school board to oversee these schools.

The parents would know what was going on at school and could spend time with their children during lunches and breaks. The teachers would be employed by the company and may have duties other than teaching. The schools would be small in small companies; however, the best classroom I ever attended as a student was with four grades in one room. One-room schools work better than the monsters we have today. Very small companies could have joint schools. Sports could be played during off hours and would be controlled by separate organizations like Little League. The older children could also learn from their parents by working part-time with them. This would give them valuable experience in the work environment and, more important, promote bonding and understanding between parents and children in a productive environment. The idea that children should not work is a family-extinguishing value. Working children bring resources to the family that can help to remove the economical disadvantage that raising children now brings to families.

This lifestyle would have many beneficial effects. The family would become a stronger unit with more mutual understanding between the members, making it happier. Parents would have more knowledge of and control over their children's environment. Drug problems would be vastly diminished. The generation gap would disappear. The social interaction between children of the opposite sexes would happen during leisure time and would not interfere with learning and healthy mental growth. Parents would always be available for the children. Parents would have an easier time with childcare and schooling. The disadvantages of being children of a two-career family would be virtually eliminated.

Companies, being profit-oriented, would run the schools more efficiently than the government. Companies have an obligation to do this since they get the most benefit from dual-career families. Teachers' pay would be on par with the rest of the work force. Women would not suffer sexual harassment and men would not suffer the tyranny of sexual harassment laws. Lesbians would have neither the advantages from co-mingling nor the disadvantages of an only-male-workers society. People might find it easier to live closer to work and families would not be going in three or more directions each day. This would ease traffic congestion, save school transportation cost, and make life easier for the entire family.

Parents who engage in the normal social interaction of raising and educating children would have the additional benefit of making connections with other people in their workplace. This would partly neutralize the disadvantages parents experience in dividing their time between home and work and their children's schools. Companies would be contributing directly to education. Everybody would be happier, especially women and children, because this life pattern is closer to the natural life pattern for the basic human animal. Mothers could stay near their small children at all times.

Of course, the public school bureaucracy will fight this idea tooth and nail because the current managers of the public schools would view this as a hostile takeover.

The first steps for allowing the new social environment would be to stop requiring co-mingling at work and allow charter schools. It is time we recognize that the present forced co-mingling in the workplace is a failure. This tyranny has been a big force in the destruction of marriages, families, and the middle class. No government that really cares about children and family would force this perverse behavior.

7. The Legal Profession

Litigation costs and the fear of being sued severely limit the activities of businesses and governments today. Awards of outrageous sums of money to people who are often more at fault than the sued institution or individual now plague our society. These lawsuits and the threat of lawsuits raise the costs families pay for almost everything and are, in large part, the result of the evolution of the legal profession.

Lawyers are not well respected in our society. They are viewed as mercenary fighters in legal battles among companies and individuals in civil cases and between governments and accused lawbreakers in criminal cases. They are viewed with disdain because they do not produce anything and appear to make a bad situation more expensive. Still, their skills with the language and their knowledge of the law and legal loopholes make them a large necessary expense in any serious legal battle. However, the legal profession is taking a much larger fraction of the country's wealth than is needed for justice to be served. Families would be better off if less money were spent on the legal profession.

Successful lawyers are not worried about justice; they are worried about the outcome of the battle. In civil suits, this translates to the most money for themselves, which means they must obtain the highest possible award for their clients. In criminal suits, the favorable verdict translates to prestige, which leads to big retainers in the future. The bottom line is still making the most money they can for themselves, in many cases with no apparent moral limitations on what they will do to get that money.

Like business, the legal profession has evolved to make more money for lawyers in a relatively direct and purposeful manner. Whoever dreams up the most effective methods of producing positive results for the client gets the biggest bucks. Unlike the evolution of institutions such as higher education and psychiatry, the legal professionals know what they are doing and why. Some individuals may pronounce themselves in business to help the innocent, but the fact is that lawyers are trained to use the law to the advantage of their clients, ignoring moral values. Public defenders, for instance, must defend the accused even if the accused is guilty. They help their clients win using any means, as long as it is legal. Morality is not an issue. This mentality exists because it keeps increasing the money going into the legal profession.

Most legal work does not involve going to trial. A disproportionate number of our politicians are lawyers, and many lawyers work with governments to obtain permission for businesses to do what they want to do. Putting up a building, selling a product, or hiring employees requires working with the government. Criminal lawyers work with governments through judges and prosecutors (all of whom are trained lawyers). If lawyers can become politically powerful, they have more influence on the government, can obtain better judgments or deals for their clients, and can then charge higher fees.

Campaigning for a political office, in addition to helping him make connections to obtain from the government what his clients want, is good publicity for a lawyer. Some law firms will lobby legislators to pass laws favorable to their clients. Their language skills help them to become successful politicians, and, since they are interested in and knowledgeable about the law, it is natural that they might want to help make the laws. Thus, lawyers tend to get into politics out of self-interest, and they have a disproportionately large representation in government. Finally, legislators hire lawyers to do the detailed writing of laws. With lawyers having such a huge influence on the laws that they are paid to manipulate for their clients, it is no surprise that litigation has become increasingly costly to society.

Over-litigation can be controlled. One way would be to prohibit lawyers and other legal professionals from running for executive or legislative offices. There is clearly a conflict of interest when lawyers are able to vote into existence the laws they will use to make money. Lawyers would still have a disproportionate influence in government through the judicial branch and through helping legislators write laws; however, if lawyers were not in the legislature, laws could be enacted to stop the explosion in litigation. The appeals process in criminal cases could be streamlined and the whole criminal justice system could be fairer and less expensive for all. Presently, lawyers are making the laws that bring them more business.

For example, it should be illegal for a lawyer to incite a client against the opposition, as is often done in divorce cases. (Mercenaries should not be allowed to incite a war.) A cap should be placed on the amount of money a lawyer can make from any one case. Family-destroying divorce would probably be less common if the lawyers made less money from it. The avoidance of inheritance tax through the use of trusts should not be allowed. (There should either be a death tax with no exceptions or not be a death tax.) Tax loopholes, in general, mostly help lawyers and accountants and the rich people they serve, while increasing the average taxpayer's expenses. The amount that can be spent to defend and the amount spent to prosecute a criminal case should be limited. This would make the system less expensive for the taxpayer and would give less advantage to the rich. In civil cases, punitive damages should not be allowed. Instead, knowingly marketing a product that puts people at excessive risk should be against the law and should be criminally prosecuted. Citizens should not be expected to punish other citizens. Punitive damages can only be justified by a vigilante mentality. This practice is presently allowed because the lawyers, who typically get about half of the booty from a lawsuit, are making the laws that allow them to get rich.

Of course, people should be allowed to sue for damages and legal expenses when they are harmed by the negligence of others; however, laws to ensure a fair but less-expensive litigation would limit the spending by both the plaintiff and the defendant. The amount that each side can spend on lawyers in civil cases might be limited to some fraction (much smaller than the present 30-60%) of the damages claimed, and the loser should pay the legal expenses for all parties. In countries outside the United States, the loser typically pays all the legal expenses. This further discourages frivolous and outrageous lawsuits.

8. Profit-Guaranteed Insurance

Insurance provides a very important service to families. Buying insurance allows us to protect ourselves financially from unlikely but ruinous events. In effect, insurance spreads the large cost of unlikely events over a large group of people so that each pays a tolerable amount of the disaster costs continuously rather than one family paying the entire cost of their own disaster. The insurance institutions collect the money as premiums from everyone and pay the cost of the disasters, while making a profit. Unfortunately, the services that insurance pays for have become excessively expensive, making insurance costs extremely burdensome to many families.

Since the insurance institutions must be large enough to spread the risk, there is a natural danger of monopoly. There is also a danger that insurance companies may collect premiums but still not have the money necessary to pay for the disasters when they happen. This is especially true for disasters that strike a large number of people simultaneously, like earthquakes and hurricanes. For these and other reasons, it became necessary for the government to regulate the insurance industry.

Insurance documents are complex and difficult to understand, and most people do not really know which things are more likely to happen to them for which they need coverage. In principle, each individual should research all the details of what he or she needs, the resources of prospective insurance companies, and the lowest premium available before he or she buys. However, this task is too onerous for the average person, and some insurance companies take unfair advantage, so some government regulation is justified. Unfortunately, like all government regulation bureaucracies, the regulating power ended up being controlled by the industry that it is supposed to be regulating. Thus, the government has organized the insurance industry into one large monopoly.

The government usually does not do its own risk assessment studies in regulating insurance premiums. Rather, it regulates the percentage of total revenues that an insurance company is allowed to take as profit. An insurance company's revenue comes from the premiums it charges for the coverage it provides. Therefore, the higher it's total premiums, the more profit an insurance company makes. Since insurance companies can only increase premiums when their claims history goes up, for the industry as a whole, the way to higher revenues and thus higher profits is ever-increasing costs of claims and resultant higher premiums. This means the most efficient way for the insurance institution to evolve, strangely enough, is to encourage large claims.

The insurance institution has contributed to the rapid cost increases in auto-body work, health care, and liability lawsuits. When a very large sum is awarded in some ridiculous lawsuit, the insurance company must pay the award; however, they are allowed to increase their premiums by more than the award, so they actually profit from the award. But the insurance companies aren't the only ones who profit. The lawyers on both sides and the plaintiff (though not as much as one might think) are big winners as well as the insurance company (the defendant). The only losers are the premium payers, and they are not at the trial. The cost-plus approach has obviously not worked because there is no incentive for the insurance industry to minimize the size of claims.

This situation has caused a double whammy in increasing the cost of health care. First, the insurance company gladly pays high healthcare costs because their allowed profits go up with the extra revenue they amass via higher premiums due to the high healthcare costs. Any procedure, no matter how ineffective or expensive, is allowed. Second, the awards in malpractice are also increasing, with the insurance companies making more profit as the awards increase and premiums go up. Because the individual doctors do not want their insurance premiums to go up, they take every conceivable precaution, which means doing every conceivable test or procedure, to protect themselves from malpractice. This further raises the cost of health care, which is again good for the insurance companies.

This bloating of cost has stimulated the growth of HMOs, which are not regulated as far as profits are concerned. HMOs can make even more profit by charging rates that are nearly as high as the insurance companies while not providing the excessive care demanded by the evolved insurance industry. The less care the HMO gives, the more profit it will make. The danger here is that, eventually, the competition between HMOs will lead to poor health care. The HMO that provides the least care will put the others out of business. This is like a non-unionized work force. The companies that pay their workforce less have a higher profit margin and put the higher paying companies out of business. This leads to low salaries for all working people, as was the case during the industrial revolution. Thus, HMOs, unless their profit schemes are changed so that their institutional evolution is carefully guided, are also going to be unsatisfactory for family survival.

The solution to the insurance problem is to approach insurance-company profits differently. The fundamental problem that is driving up the cost of everything that is insured is the regulation of profits instead of the standardization of the product. Presently, each company offers a different policy (that is, different coverage combinations), which makes it very difficult for people to read all the fine print to compare costs in the light of coverage.

Either the industry or the government should standardize the insurance policies with only a very few numbers that define the level of coverage and a few different types of policies. Then all companies would have the same policies and comparison-shopping would be simple, leading to fairer competition and natural price controls. Companies that consistently lose or settle high-award lawsuits would go out of business because their premiums would be higher than those who consistently fight for the lowest awards. The government would still dictate the assets that an insurance company must have on hand in order to offer various numbers of various policies.

In summary, the government should require the standardization of the products within each insurance category (auto, health, business, malpractice, etc.) so people can easily shop around for insurance. They should also make sure the companies have the assets they need to payout when a loss occurs. Finally, as in any industry, the government would make sure there are enough independent companies so that there is real competition.

Clearly, lawyers benefit from the high litigation costs stimulated by cost-plus government regulations and the determination of blame and who's going to pay. It follows that the first step in improving the situation is the removal of lawyers from the law-making business as discussed in the previous chapter.

9. Summary of Actions to Control Institutions

We certainly do not need to destroy our institutions; however, we do need to change the rules so that their evolution will be to support the survival of families. The following is a summary of changes discussed throughout the book that might reverse the negative trends outlined in the preface. These ideas are suggestions that might be tried for a while to see the effect. The new rules might have glitches that will trigger some other pathological evolution requiring further modification; however, the problem with the present situation is not that institutional evolution is pathological, it's that no one is trying to identify the pathology and change the patterns of evolution to cure the pathology.

We must change the funding rules so that higher education receives more money when alumni have replacement children. BEEism would then evolve so that it instills family-survival values instead of the anti-family values it instills today. Colleges and universities should be required to publish data on the domestic success of each institution's alumni so parents can judge the effective sterilization rate of colleges and universities while choosing an institution of higher education for their children. Tuition should be tax deductible and donations should not be tax deductible. Endowments and income from endowments should be taxed. The government should forgive education loans as graduates have children and give financial incentives to universities that produce domestically successful alumni. An extreme solution might be to disallow childless alumni from contributing to their alma mater. The universities should receive education grants from the government based on the number of students they graduate with acceptable scores on competency tests. We must work hard to eliminate righteous arguments and censorship while encouraging intellectual discussions on campus.

Psychiatrists should contract, with patients and their families, specific fees per diagnosis and/or treatment instead of working for hourly rates. Close family members should accompany patients to "sessions", and any findings that appear to be "caused by" someone other than the patient should be discussed with that person as part of the patient's treatment. Specifically, family members should be allowed the opportunity to defend themselves.

We need to get back to allowing physical affection, physical reward, and physical punishment in the rearing of children, especially boys.

Federal district judges should be elected within their districts, and the state governments should have legal input to Supreme Court appointments. We should consider returning to each state's legislature the appointment, rather than the popular election, of its *U.S.* Senators.

The power of the President as Commander in Chief should be greatly reduced unless war is declared by Congress. The use of our military by the President for domestic political purposes must be stopped. We need to cut the size of the military because it is more powerful than we need and our families need the excess money. Wasting the excess in unneeded wars like Iraq actually damages our position in the world.

Management positions should be removed from the Federal Civil Service system and revert to appointed positions, with only the lowest level positions being career bureaucrats. This would give control of the government back to elected officials while preserving the operation of the government during administration changes. The heads of powerful bureaucracies like the FBI and CIA should only be allowed to serve for short times, with no renewals of appointments.

The right of law-abiding citizens to bear arms should not be infringed. The existence of firearms should be treated as an everyday course of life, and classes in the proper use and care of firearms should be taught in public schools, just as personal hygiene and driver's education are now taught.

Because of the sense of power and importance it promotes, it should be illegal to publish the name or picture of murders and other violent criminals.

The Federal Government must be taken out of family relations. We must stop the taxation for the care of the elderly through Social Security and stop giving retirement saving, as opposed to personal saving, special preferential tax treatment. The family should be able to keep wealth with the children using it to manage the care of their parents. Children would then be taught respect for the old and to take care of their elderly parents. In light of this future caregiving, people would raise their children with greater love, respect, and diligence. This return to mutual nurturing would help to remove the present disadvantages to reproduction that are extinguishing many families in industrialized countries. A fraction of the income tax paid by children should be returned to their parents, as a financial return on their childrearing investment, to reinforce mutual nurturing.

Bureaucracies should be redesigned or set up so they grow as the problems they are designed to address are solved. A list of goals along with the monetary reward or punishment could be used to make this happen. This method takes advantage of the fact that bureaucracies will grow.

The present welfare system and income tax system needs to be replaced with a guaranteed-income and flat-tax (GIFT) system administered by the IRS. This system provides a survival income for all adult citizens but not enough to replace employment income or care provided by children and/or savings for a comfortable old age. The tax system would have incentives for employment as well as the survival of all families. Social Security and the Department of Health and Human Services would be replaced with GIFT, greatly decreasing the size (and therefore the expense) of government.

Women need to be removed from dangerous jobs like criminal apprehension, fire fighting, and combat. This may stop the present evolution toward cowardly policies in such occupations. We should recognize that some jobs are inherently dangerous and being super-safe on the job is unnecessary and can defeat the purpose of some of those jobs—protecting others from harm.

Through research and education, we should work toward legalizing drugs, eliminating the prescription-drug monopoly, and redesign the FDA Bureaucracy to be more family-friendly and less big-business friendly.

We can minimize violence by reversing elitist policies that create an oppressed subclass. The majority of American citizens are intelligent enough to make their own decisions.

Tough sentences for criminals and "three strikes, you're out" laws should be used to decrease crime and decrease the cost of law enforcement.

Everything possible should be done to keep children with their natural parents, whose authority must not be undermined. Abortions should be controlled by state laws, not the Supreme Court, and should not happen without "due process". Abortion laws and other unjust laws concerning domestic relations need to be changed. We must stop subsidizing and encouraging divorce.

All forms of entertainment should be rated concerning their potential impact on people's values, such as positive or negative feelings they instill about persons in authority, blacks, marriage, parents, schooling, etc. Presently only the "eye candy" is rated, such as levels of sex and violence. To prevent our perceptions of reality from being destroyed, we must limit our consumption of fiction, especially TV and movies, and become educated about its propaganda messages.

The use of the power of TV and movies should be severely limited in politics. For example, audio only or still pictures only are all that should be allowed on TV for political discourse so that the rest of the brain can focus on thinking logically about what is being seen or heard. The media needs to be broken up to stop it from being controlled by so few like-thinking people. These actions would help to break the stranglehold the media presently has on our politics and our government. New political parties should be given more opportunity through voter ranking of candidates instead of a simple "pick-one" vote.

We must realize that free trade is really the transfer of power from the people to business. The media is leading this globalization, which, following institution evolution, will eventually lead to a very tyrannical world government.

For the sake of marriage and children, we should stop co-mingling men and women in the workplace. Businesses that hire women should be required to have a nursery and a school for girls on site. Businesses that hire men should be required to have a school for boys on site. The older boys and girls should work alongside their same-sex parent when they are not in class. The schools would be run by the parents but paid for and overseen by the state and the business.

It should be illegal for lawyers to become legislators or government executives because of the conflict of interest. Lawyers in the executive and legislative branches of government stack the deck in favor of the legal industry. Getting the lawyers out of the law-making business will lower the excessive cost society now pays for litigation. For example, punitive damages in civil suits should be eliminated in lieu of criminal prosecution and stronger sentences, and costs of litigation should be limited. The losers in lawsuits should pay all the legal fees, which should also be limited.

The government should standardize insurance policies so that competition is possible and stop tying insurance-company profits to a percentage of revenue.

Presently there are a number of very powerful institutions that are continuing to rapidly grow in power while decreasing the freedom, wealth, and power of our families. Consequently, many of our best family lines are being greatly damaged and even extinguished. The next generation has been decimated and is being reared very poorly. If these institutions are not stopped, the American experiment will fail in a couple of generations. Surviving families will again be mostly slaves to tyrannical rulers. However, the people still have control of the government in the U.S.A., in that the votes are mostly being counted and the elected politicians are mostly good people. Therefore, we must start now to reverse this evolution, for it will become more difficult the longer we delay. The first step is for people to understand that it is happening and it can be reversed. The main purpose of this book is to help with this first step.

Changing the rules for institutions so they support the survival of families will be difficult and will take considerable time and effort. However, there is one strong force on the side of the families: immoral values that extinguish families generally die out because those that hold the values usually only last a generation. For example, the plot below shows that the family-extinguishing values of the Democratic Party are the Party's own undoing.

The Democrats are losing the cultural war because they are literally killing themselves. The plot has two curves. The solid curve represents the number of voters from 1992 onward that were killed by legal abortion. (It is the number of abortions since *Roe vs. Wade* that would have voted had they lived, assuming 50% would have voted.) The dashed curve is the number of additional votes the Democrats would have needed to maintain the lead they had in the 1992 Presidential election. If you discount Dole in 1996 as a serious candidate (dip in need) and assume the possibility that the aborted people would have voted Democratic (like their parents) then you can say the Democrats' losses in 2000 and 2004 were caused by *Roe vs. Wade*. While this does not prove that abortions caused the losses, it does show that the number of aborted voters is sufficient to have changed the outcome of these elections.

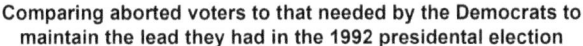

Comparing aborted voters to that needed by the Democrats to
maintain the lead they had in the 1992 presidental election

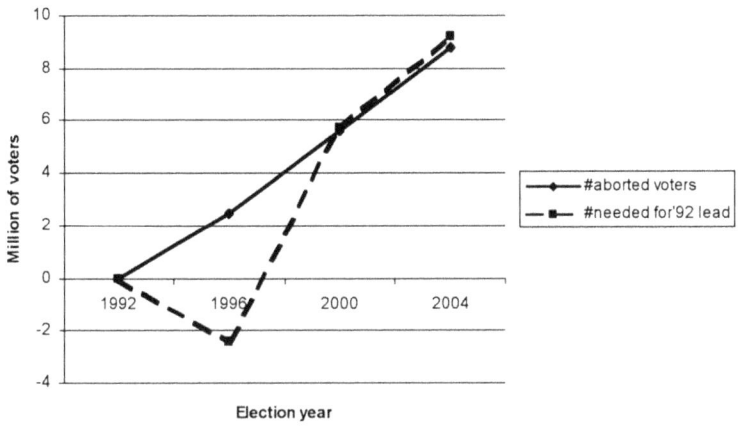

In addition to fanatic pro-abortion values, other family-extinguishing
values the Democrats need to shed are a) the gay life style is great, b)
men and women have identical responsibility in being wage earners
and in being homemakers, and c) humans are the scourge of the
earth. All of these immoral values also indirectly yet very powerfully
denigrate motherhood, which is an extremely family-extinguishing
effect.   In addition, the Democrats discourage reproduction by
undermining parental authority through supporting the stealing of
children from people that are suspected of not raising them like the
government thinks they should. The tragedy is the families that have
been extinguished because they believed these immoral values are
moral. Ideas that extinguish families eventually, literally, die out with
the families they extinguish.   Unfortunately, some of our best and
most educable families are being extinguished and our country might
die before the anti-family values die. We cannot be complacent and
allow this to happen.

We need to change the Democratic Party by removing the BEE
litmus tests in all states and by making true advocacy for real families

and restraint of big business its first priority. The 2006 and 2008 campaigns appear to be steps in the right direction.

Finally, we must teach our children family-survival values and the source of anti-family values. We need to strengthen the value of mutual nurturing and the importance of having children. Parents should offset the financial cost of grandchildren by leaving their estate primarily to children that are producing grandchildren. This also keeps the family wealth in the family.

10. Appendix: Human Animalistic Instincts and the American Experiment

The following discussion is based on the observation of human relations in primitive people and in other isolated groups of humans, such as cults; on the observation of herd animals that are at the top of the food chain; and on the observation of other omnivorous primates.

The uncivilized human is a pack animal that lives in a tribe with an alpha-male leader that takes on a semi-deity position. He assumes the role because he is considered the best or strongest individual in the tribe. He has sexual rights with his choice of females, and as he grows in alpha power, he goes through hormonal changes that increase his sexual activities, a phenomenon we see in our leaders today. As Henry Kissinger once said, "Power is the ultimate aphrodisiac". This exploitation of the reproduction of the best and healthiest maximizes evolution for the survival of the tribe and the species as a whole.

In the early days, survival was touch-and-go, and maximum evolution to support survival was necessary. Beside defending against the outside physical threats of wild animals and other men, hunting and other activities designated as men's work were led by the alpha-male. Undoubtedly, the hormonal changes the alpha-male experienced made him stronger and better in other ways as well. Until recently, evolution was about the only solution to disease, and it is still the only permanent solution. Without the intervention of medicine, the susceptible die and the survivors reproduce. With the intervention of medicine, the susceptible survive, reproduce, and their susceptible offspring must deal with the disease over and over again.

While the alpha-male rules supreme, the alpha-female does exercise some control over him. Evolution has given him an innate desire to keep the females happy, healthy, and secure, especially the ones with whom he has sexually bonded. Secure and healthy females are essential for the reproduction of the tribe. The alpha-female is the leader of the females of the tribe. She leads the women in activities that are designated as women's work. One of the primary functions of the alpha-female is to keep harmony within the tribe. The males are the soldiers and killers. The women keep the men from killing each other. The alpha-female stays informed of all of the internal tribal activities and interactions, and she controls the alpha-male as necessary to promote the security and tranquility of the tribe. The continuity of the tribe depends on the females, since the males are often killed and the alpha-male frequently changes. Minimizing the carnage that accompanies the change of the dominant male helps the growth and survival of the tribe.

The alpha-male is not the only male reproducing, especially in large tribes. His lieutenants, the elite, are allowed different levels of sexual freedom with the females, depending on how valuable to the tribe the other male is considered. Also, the most valuable members are the last to die in difficult times. The females that are attracted to and accepted by the alpha-male and the elite lieutenants have a better chance for survival because they are able to obtain more resources from the tribe for themselves and their offspring. The females that are considered the most attractive are most likely to become mates of the more powerful males. If the female is on good terms with the alpha-female, her perceived value in the tribe and her attractiveness are increased. A female's attractiveness, and thus security, is improved if she understands and obeys the tribal rules. Thus, women that appear to obey the rules, try to be attractive, and are attracted to powerful males tend to survive.

Since the elite males have more than one female mate, many males are left without mates. The low-class males, low in the pecking order, are highly controlled by the dominant males and have very little freedom. If a male is doomed to the lowest class, he does not have a mate. The best thing he can do to reproduce is to form a conspiracy with others in a similar situation and either take over the tribe or leave the tribe to form a new pack. The new pack will then try to find females that are so poorly protected that they can be abducted and assimilated into the pack to form a new tribe. Low-status females of the original tribe might voluntarily join the revolt if they have a chance of having high status in the new tribe. Obviously, males desiring freedom and power tend to be more successful at reproduction. Since one male can take care of the reproductive needs of many females, the females have little difficulty finding a mate. Therefore, rather than needing freedom and power to be reproductive, females need security and enough power to assure the resources to protect and nurture themselves and their children.

This system allowed uncivilized man to adapt rapidly against new diseases or other changes in the environment that threatened his extinction. The mating of a few of the best and healthiest males with all the females enabled a much more rapid evolution than our monogamous system. Thus, this system dominated for millions of years.

Other human characteristics also developed under this system. A keen sensitivity to conspiracy helped the elite keep the reproductive position. Better to investigate ten false conspiracies than to let one real one go unnoticed. A male that jealously protected his females from other males was more likely to have offspring. On the other hand, a female who secretly developed relationships with potential future leaders increased her chances of survival when a change in the alpha-male occurred.

The supremacists needed the oppressed to do the dirty work; however, the oppressed often outnumbered the supremacists. Very often, when the oppressed gained the upper hand, they killed a large number of the deposed hated supremacists. They then, of course, became the new supremacists. This still happens today, and was most recently demonstrated in Rwanda, where the oppressed Hutus murdered the supremacist Tutsis. The Holocaust was "justified" in their opinion as the extinguishing of deposed supremacists by previously oppressed people. The hatred of government or authority figures today comes from this natural hatred of supremacists by the oppressed.

The elitists' feelings of superiority and their abuse of the subservient, as well as the strong hatred of the elite by the abused, are animalistic instincts that were very effective in fighting disease. Their strong hatred gave the healthy oppressed the strength and will to take over as soon as a new disease weakened the elite. The killing of the weakened elite quickly halted reproduction of the non-resistant genes.

The tribes that worked hard to grow and to become more powerful and more secure were the most successful in populating the earth. Thus, the desire to increase the size of the tribe and increase its resources has strong survival value to the human animal. This is especially important for the alpha-males and females, since they have the greatest genetic investment in the tribe.

Our basic human characteristics were developed through millions of years in the tribal situation described above, and the several thousand years of intervening, contrasting, advanced large civilizations have not had time to evolve us away from these basic drives and needs. Not only has the "civilized" time frame been relatively short, but the remaining basic characteristics do not have strong negative survival value even in the most civilized environments. Here are some important animal characteristics of humans:

1. People strive to make the tribe or close group grow in number, security, strength, and resources.
2. Individuals strive to appear valuable to the tribe and to achieve a high-level position.
3. Freedom is more important to men, while security is more important to women.

4. Women strive to be attractive and to appear to obey the rules, while men strive to appear powerful, to command resources, and to acquire respect.
5. People tend to form elitist groups and attempt to gain power and control over others who, in turn, hate them for it.

Although the animal state of man was probably optimal for evolving to combat disease and other perils of a harsh, uncontrolled environment, it was not a very happy situation. The alpha-male and his elitist lieutenants were always in fear of a conspiracy that would demote or kill them. The underclass was without mates, lacked the freedom to pursue happiness, and was consumed by hatred for the elite. The women lived in fear of losing the resources they needed to raise their children and, indeed, of losing everything in the carnage of leadership change. They used the power of their sexual attractiveness to carry on secret affairs with potential new leaders so they could survive a change, knowing that it meant death if the affairs were discovered. The American experiment is an attempt to make a happier environment for humans.

In the American experiment, all men are equal lieutenants under God, the eternal benevolent ruler. Coupling this concept with the tradition of monogamy, the unmated underclass is nearly completely eliminated. Each woman can have a lieutenant to serve her and provide the love, resources, security, and protection she needs for herself and her children, with no chance of (ultimate) leadership change. She, in turn, gives her mate the power, dignity, and fidelity he needs to confirm his lieutenant status, all of which makes him reasonably happy. Following God prevents either from turning into overbearing alphas. All are given their freedom and security by the only and eternal alpha, God. All humans have equal and full value because, and only because, they are human and humans are valuable to God. Since the value Almighty God places on him or her is all that matters to each human, no one feels smaller or less valuable if he or she happens to have less money or intelligence or physical beauty. The administrators of the government are elected to serve the people, with God as their master, and are not considered superior to anyone else. (Politicians sometimes have trouble controlling their sex drive because they undergo a hormonal change caused by thinking of themselves—rather than God—as the rulers). Considering the limitations of the basic nature of the human animal, this is about as close to Utopia as we can get.

Unfortunately, this experiment is beginning to fail rather rapidly because of institution evolution. We must recognize and combat this problem to stop our backward slide toward the unhappy, more primitive state of an elitist ruling class and a mateless, revolutionary underclass.

The evolution of the animalistic human into the American experiment went through several stages. One characteristic that separates humans from animals is the ability to reason and to believe in God. Early humans recognized God but did not recognize the equality of all humans in God's eyes. Nonetheless, the worship of a misconstrued God allowed the units of human organization to grow from small tribes, ruled and controlled by the alpha-male and alpha-female, to large countries where peace within the country or culture is maintained by a growing belief in God and a common worship and morality.

Unfortunately, because different people are at different stages in their belief in God, elitism still raises its ugly head, and some countries and cultures consider themselves the chosen people, praying to their god for the power to conquer the other "lesser" peoples so they can take their god-given place as the elite. Belief in God has been perverted into the belief that some chosen individuals have the "divine" right to rule as monarchs and then to extend their kingdoms as they see fit. Even today, there are primitive religions that fail to recognize the full dignity of the humans who are outside of their religions, teaching that people inside the religion are truly superior and should lead the rest of the lesser humanity. Of course, these types of religions generate great conflicts throughout the world.

There are also political leaders who add the evil of elitism to good religions to achieve the same effect as the primitive religions. Many people today see the conflicts generated by this abuse of religion and conclude that religion is bad, but they're wrong. Religion is good and powerful, but it can be poisoned and misdirected, often by the animalistic instinct of elitism. Religions that include elitism as part of the dogma, no matter how evolved they may appear, are actually primitive religions and anti-American.

ABOUT THE AUTHOR

The author received his bachelor degree from the University of Illinois and then attended graduate school at the University of California, Berkeley during the Vietnam War protest period, earning a Ph.D. He married while in graduate school. Following employment for over a decade at the Los Alamos National Laboratory, where he had become a group leader, he became a professor at the University of Washington. He is, over nineteen years later, a successful teacher and researcher and receives considerable research funding from the Federal Government. He has many publications in peer-reviewed scientific journals. His background has made him very familiar with the workings of universities and the Federal Government. He was divorced and remarried. He has five children and eight grandchildren.

CPSIA information can be obtained
at www.ICGtesting.com
Printed in the USA
BVHW091823110522
636755BV00006B/573

9 781439 240038